TABLE OF CONTENTS

INTRODUCTION

Things To Consider When Planning To Build A Greenhouse In Your Home Garden

considering a greenhouse. It's a major investment that should be planned ahead of time. With a lot of considerations needed to be addressed, it's hard to know where to start. But today, we will take things little by little by laying out the basic guidelines, breaking up the basic necessities and giving you pro tips that include budgeting, choosing an ideal location as well as weather considerations. Whether you are a beginner or a seasoned professional, you will surely get fresh ideas from this article on how to thing to consider when planning to build a greenhouse in your home garden.

The Perfect Location

There may be only one possible location to put a greenhouse in your garden. But if you do have the options, it's well worth giving the possible best position you can. With careful site selection, you will optimize the productivity of your greenhouse structure which helps you offset the space it takes up in your garden, the time and effort spent in building one as well as your initial outlay.

You will need a location that has the most exposure to solar radiation.

Your plants need at least six hours exposure to sunlight for photosynthesis. The process is necessary for plants to grow healthy and bear fruits or flower. The best sitting direction largely depends on the season you want to grow plants.

East-West Facing Ridge. Lining up the ridge of the structure to run east to west maximize light interception especially during November to January. The direction will help crops heat up more quickly after cold nights.

South Facing Ridge. This sitting position is preferable only if you intend to grow your crops during summer. The direction will distribute will generate an equal amount of light to each side of the structure and helps reduce too much heat temperature.

Further Note: If possible, avoid the north side part of your home as the plants are limited by the amount of sunlight in this area unless you are willing to facilitate additional source of light and heat. Also, keep in mind that shadowy areas will limit the necessary amount of sunlight your greenhouse will receive. Shade lines differ between summer and winter. It is advised that a greenhouse should be at a distance equal to at least twice the height of any potential shade source.

Recent research also suggests that a site's latitude should be a basis of your preferred orientation on your structure. For example, for southern latitudes where there is a warmer temperature, a north-south orientation is ideal to provide good light and best ventilation. Further, the strength and direction of the wind should also be considered. Outdoor gardening is quite challenging on windy areas. Opt for a spot where you will have a wind-proof such as trees but make sure it doesn't cause too much shadowing

Make sure the site has an easy access to water, electricity and other needed utilities. You will want a location that is near to water access, heat and electricity for convenient gardening. The watering system is essential in gardening especially that a natural source of water such as rain or groundwater is restricted. In laying out one, it is best to study your land profile. Better yet, choose a spot where you can lay out your water irrigation successfully. This also works the same for the electricity needed in lawn mowers, hedge trimmers along with providing power with outdoor lights, pond pumps and greenhouse heaters. Care must be taken to avoid fire and electrocution.

A stable elevated ground is necessary to prevent unnecessary water accumulation. While watering is an essential for the growth of plants, they can also suffer or die from overwatering that mainly cause by rain flood or extra waters coming off the roof. It is best to build your structure to an elevated ground so runoff flows away from the greenhouse smoothly.

Further Note: It is technically possible to orient a greenhouse on a slope but avoid doing so. You will need a higher elevated ground but putting it in a base of a slope will frost pocket where coldness lingers, especially for winter farming.

Find a site where there is a decent soil to grow plants or the potential to become so. If you are not quite sure of the soil's profile, you will need to hire an expert to analyze the nutrient, texture, and composition of your land's soil. Poor soil can be improved by digging in organic matter. But unless you will be able to find an area that has excellent gardening soil and natural drainage, little preparation is required when it comes to cultivating it, reducing weed seed bank and adding organic matter.

Further Note: Try to avoid stony or rocky ground as it can be a hiccup in the construction process.

Lastly, a location's capability of expansion is also nice. The need for expansion is always unpredictable. In the future, you may need a larger space for your growing crops or you may need an increase the number of your plants. It is always ideal to build a greenhouse in a large area to cater to the possibility of expansion.

THE ALLOCATION OF SPACE

How much space are you going to need? As mentioned, your chosen location should provide you ample room for expansion for years to come. In addition, the allocated space should justify the borrowed space in your garden. In many instances, greenhouse owners either end up having that extra space they seldom need or wanting more of the square footage. In avoiding these common mistakes, it is necessary to evaluate the factors that commonly take up space in a greenhouse.

The Plants You Want to Fit In. Initially, a compact space is used for seed planting. As plants grow, you will need to triple the space. A 10' x 10' is usually the minimum size for potted plants. But less space is required for greenhouses with cabin fevers. In fact, even a 6' x 6' is already a treat. For bedding plant farming where gardeners grew plants on the floor, it is necessary to leave enough walking aisle to place 1-foot at least in front of the other. When production time arrives, you can have that working aisle by harvesting the plant first on center area.

Aisles, Walkways and Working Space. It is a common

practice to leave enough walking space to observe and harvest plants. Normally, 40 percent of the floor area is for aisles and walkways. With at least 18-inch work aisles between and one three to five-foot main aisle down the center, you will potentially increase growing space by at least 10 percent. This method also provides easy access for moving plants with cart.

Bonus Tip: One meter of space all around the structure is necessary not only for putting up easier access to the greenhouse but also useful in such cases where maintenance issues arise. For example, it will be easier to replace panes or covers or cleaning if you have allocated enough space for walking past. Leaving this space will also mean that fences and other structures are not close enough to block ventilation or cast unwanted shade. Leaving generous space on the front is also wise as the opening door is another way for ventilation and air circulation.

Benches, Racks, Hanging Baskets. These are all extras but also can make the most of the space. Benches are normally used to utilize space for the production area. It works well for crops such as ground cover. 60-90 percent of conventional, lengthwise benches typically contributes to the floor area. Configuration wise, movable trays are more efficient. Other choose to hang baskets to increase space utilization. Hanging basket conveyor are attached to the overhead trusses where plants are spaced eight-inch apart. For larger potted plants, an A-frame rack system can double your growing space. They can be built within 2' x 4' lumber and fence pipe or with heavy steel rods. However, if you just need something to put off your plants from the ground, shelves will do the pinch and are boxy to small spaces.

Irrigation and Drainage. These two factors can eat up space. Drip irrigation won't be a problem for large and big greenhouses, but for a smaller setup, one may be able to efficiently use hand watering. Meanwhile, floor drainage should start with a six to eight-inch gravel or stone base under the floor.

THE KIND OF PLANTS YOU WANT TO GROW

If you are new to gardening, it's best to have ideas on what plants that will grow best in your greenhouse. This will depend heavily on your setup as well as the capability of your greenhouse to control environmental factors. However, suitable plants for greenhouse gardening are available for every kind of greenhouse and climate. They are grouped into three categories; Vegetable and Crops, Fruits and Ornamentals.

Vegetables and Crops

For beginners, it's wiser to start with easy vegetables so that within a year you can get a grip on the basics of growing one. As you a get hands on them you can continue with the complex crops. Here are some examples of easy-to-grow plants in your greenhouse.

Leafy Vegetables. Veggies that belongs to that of 'salad family' such as lettuce grows in the same manner, especially when considering the bedding plants.

Peppers. Nearly every variety of peppers can grow well in a greenhouse. They are best placed in a minimum of 15 inches apart and temperatures consistency of above 55 degrees Fahrenheit.

Tomatoes: With ample sunlight and a stable night temperature of at least 55 degrees Fahrenheit, tomatoes can grow exceptionally well in greenhouses.

Microgreens. Packed with nutritional punch, microgreens are ideal for family-oriented greenhouses. These are the tiny tender version of familiar vegetables. Growers like to diversify them by taking varieties such as brassicas, arugula or spicy-type-greens. They germinate them and let these tiny crops grow out for a week or two.

Herbs. Most of the seed-bearing plants are perhaps the easiest ones to grow. Germinating and raising them to require little attention. As long as you have a good control over the temperature of your greenhouse, you won't encounter any problems growing them. Common popular herbs in greenhouses include basil, cilantro, tarragon, rosemary and thyme

Other Warm Season Vegetables. These summer crops require a high intensity of at least 60 degrees Fahrenheit during daytime and a minimum 55 degrees Fahrenheit at night. Several varieties of vegetable within this classification do well in a greenhouse. These include beans, cucumbers, eggplants, cantaloupe and summer squash.

Other Cold Season Vegetables. Winter vegetables are best to grow in greenhouses since they fail to pollinate in warm temperatures. These crops require a daytime temperature range of 50-70 degrees Fahrenheit and 45-55 degrees Fahrenheit at night. Beets, cabbage, cauliflower, broccoli, carrots, chard, turnips, peas, and radishes are among this cold season vegetables.

Fruits

Growing fruits demands a warm environment. Most fruit trees appreciate temperatures above 50 degrees Fahrenheit while above 60 Fahrenheit for tropical fruits. But even in unheated greenhouses, a range of fruits can all be raised in surprisingly undemanding ways.

Citrus Fruits. You can grow a variety of oranges, lemons, and tangerines in greenhouses. They have the ability to sustain even the coldest weather. They only need a temperature around 55 degrees Fahrenheit for them to germinate and survive winter.

Peaches and Nectarines. Newbies normally prefers peaches as they are nourishing and simple to handle. Together with nectarines, both can be grown in either unheated or cool greenhouse.

Grapes. Growing vines invariably call for high temperatures. With proper ventilation and heating, a greenhouse can be a perfect place to grow grapes. Some varieties of grapes can also thrive inside a cooler temperature, such are Black Hamburgh and Buckland Sweetwater.

Further Note: Grapevines require a lot of room. One vine is, in fact, plenty for a small greenhouse. One meter should be allocated between each vine. It is important to evaluate if growing one will be invasive to your garden space.

ORNAMENTALS

Ornamentals are in demand and can be a good source of income. It beautifies a landscape and can also be a decorative addition to any home. Whatever your reason for growing one, you will surely find a range of ornamentals that do excellent in any kind of greenhouses.

Flower-Bearing Plants. One of the benefits of having a greenhouse is having the chance to produce blooming plants all year round. With the use of appropriate lightings and solar heating, you will be able to grow some of the most exciting and colorful flowers.

Sun or Shade-Loving Annuals: These graceful ornamentals bear gorgeous pendulous flowers making them ideal for hanging baskets. The petal-filled blooms appear in a number of shades and some selections offer variegated foliage. Each season, gardeners come out with few or more varieties of shade flowers. Among the favorites are Alyssum, Begonia, Lady's Eardrop, Impatiens, Hypoestes and Angel Wing Caladiums.

Perennials: These stem flowers are your best sources of fresh cut flowers. Compared to annual plants, perennials can grow for two seasons and flourish exceptionally when grown in a greenhouse because of its ideal regulated temperatures. Normally the plants are grown in a greenhouse during winter and are brought outdoors to fill the garden in summer. The popular arrays that make a perennial garden are Anemone, Tulip Bulbs, Lilies, Asters, Chrysanthemums, Daisies, Gaillardias, Roses, and Hyacinth.

Shrubs and Climbers. Some of these varieties cannot be grown successfully in an open garden and need the protection of a greenhouse. True climbers take up little ground space and are excellent choices for smaller greenhouses while wall shrubs require more ground space. Popular plants are Clematis, Shrub Roses, Wisteria, and Honeysuckle.

Tropicals. Even tropical plants that require hotter temperature can have a place in a greenhouse. If you want to grow something more diverse, greenhouses can be an ideal setting for tropical plants like cacti, orchids, Venus flytraps and other carnivorous plants, providing that you pay close attention to the indoor conditions.

TYPES OF GREENHOUSES

The type of greenhouse you need depends on where you live and what you want to grow. From functionality to aesthetics, greenhouses are now also being built-up according to design and style. Following are the inspiring greenhouses you may want to consider categorized based on environmental temperature needs, functionality, appearance, and construction.

According to Temperature

Cold Houses (Temperature: below freezing). The method is to start crops early in fall and extend the growing season in spring. It still provides protection for plants despite having no additional heat source.

Cool Houses (Temperature: 45-50F). The design is driven by creating a space that is able to capture as much light and heat from the sun as possible. The heat is redistributed during the night time so that plants that can't adapt to extreme cold can still survive.

Warm Houses (Temperature: 55F). These greenhouses are particularly designed to operate during the coldest times of the year when sunlight is at a minimum. It provides protection for plants from adverse weather through a transparent roof enclosure normally built low to the ground. The primary function is to allow a broader range of plants to survive.

Hot Houses (Temperature: 60F). This type install supplemental heat. Hot houses are often used to grow tropical plants.

According to Design or Structure

Plethora of designs are available to choose from but the following are most common types use.

A-Frame. A vented roof and side walls are the design's prominent feature. The key advantage is the minimization of materials that just enough to meet the requirements of the greenhouse productivity.

Gothic Arch. Beyond its state-of-the-art curved roof, a Gothic Arch is well known to resist extreme temperatures. It includes a semicircular frame of either galvanized pipe or conduit and is usually covered with plastic.

Conventional or Post and Rafter. The embedded post and rafters are among the strongest design to support the roof. It maximizes the space usage and provides efficient air circulation.

Freestanding. The growing need for a greenhouse that can be moved or removed gives rise to freestanding greenhouses. This type of greenhouse, as the name suggests, stands independently which lets you place or move them wherever you please. The materials could be a set of hoops that are covered with plastic or frame that runs on rails or skids that can be moved with a tractor or winches. This type is ideal for greenhouses only operates during on a specific season like summer or winter, a freestanding greenhouse is your best bet as it can be removed and put back again conveniently.

MATERIALS AND CONSTRUCTION

A greenhouse construction can involve glazing, framing, and laying out the basic foundation. The construction is something you want to last as long as possible to avoid costly repair works. Choosing the best quality materials to support your structure's strong and sturdy construction is your next big step.

The Foundation

After spotting in that perfect location, the first material you'll be working with will be the foundation. Choosing the suitable foundation is the tricky part in constructing a greenhouse because this component is critical to the stability of the structure and will be responsible in anchoring it in place. You have two options with the materials but the decision should be dependent on the size and location of your greenhouse as well as your budget.

Wood. Choosing wood as a foundation is one of the economical ways of building greenhouses. It is inexpensive a stable foundation. The simplest and most common type is made from pressure treated wood that is a great option for small greenhouses. Resistant woods such as cedar, redwood, and cypress are popular because they contain substances that inhibit decay. As for the styles, railroad ties and platform construction are common choices for good drainage.

Concrete. This type of foundation is highly recommended for colder climates as it helps eliminate the effects of the ground freeze of the structure. A concrete foundation provides a very stable and secure base that will certainly last you for a period of time requires little maintenance. That is if you set it up right. Building one requires more experience and knowledge in pouring, leveling and smoothing concrete. If you find this method more of a challenge, you can always hire trained laborers to do it for you.

Further note: In building a greenhouse foundation, it is necessary to level the ground after removing sods and weeds. It is also very important to evaluate your building codes before building a foundation. You may need a specific permit or there may be a zoning law that prohibits particular foundation. Alternatively, there may also be a rule that allows you to only you a certain type of foundation.

FRAMING

Next up, you'll be taking a look at the materials that are going to be in the actual frame or 'skeleton' of your greenhouse. Frameworks are necessary to support the construction of the structure. As to what kind of material to use can depend on your chosen covering or glazing. Heavier glazing requires aheavier frame. Here are some materials you may want to consider.

Wood. This is the most common sought material when it comes to insulation and ease of assembly. However, it is important to opt for redwood, cedar or treated woods as other types can result to wood warps when once damp or wet. Wood can also last you quite long in dry climates with proper upkeep.

Aluminum. This low maintenance material doesn't rust and has tolerance to natural elements such as solar radiation and water. It might not be the strongest, but it provides a good rigid form for glass or polycarbonate coverings.

Galvanized Steel. Durable and inexpensive, galvanized steels require fewer frameworks because the material has strong solid components. However, there should be a proper maintenance as steels can wear and rust.

Polyvinyl Chloride (PVC) Plastic. The best benefit a PVC plastic can offer is limited heat loss that is ideal for greenhouses that operate during winter seasons. They are lightweight, portable and easy to assemble. With this kind of framing, you have to be cautious in choosing covering options. Due to its lightweight, it can only be able to support a lightweight covering.

Odds and Ends

The difference between an average greenhouse and a greenhouse that will last you a lifetime can be determined by the added materials that lend stability. Reinforcing odds and ends are just extras but will help your structure go that extra mile. Following are small additions you may want to consider giving your greenhouse that ultimate strength.

Trussing. Long rods reinforced at the tops insides of framing ribs makes frameworks sturdier. These rods run on each side of rib arches joining them together so the standing structure will less likely to fall over even with extreme wind and adverse weather.

Small Beams. These are added to the frame or foundation to lend similar stability. It can be of wood or metal.

Anchors. Cables that is either tied to weights or staked down straight to the ground are added to weigh down the entire structure. This is normally done after glazing the greenhouse. With the added construction, the greenhouse can withstand high winds and storms more.

End Walls. Additional end frames and doors secures a firm and built to last greenhouses.

GLAZING OR COVERING

Layering the greenhouse cover is the final touch. As mentioned, choosing the type of materials for the panels should be based on the frame setup and vice versa. Additionally, choosing the glazing materials as well as how many layers needed also depend on the amount of insulation.

Glass. Beyond its aesthetic appeal, glass glazing offers great light transmission than any commonly used glazing. It's a no-brainer that glass structures are fragile. Nonetheless, repair issues that mostly caused by projectiles like hailstones less likely happen.

Plastic. This glazing is lighter and flexible than glass. They are available in larger panes, reducing drafts and making construction easier. Fiberglass is one type of plastic glazing that has a gel coat for UV protection, retaining heat better than glass. Polycarbonate is also a corrugated plastic that is almost as transparent as glass but wears longer than fiberglass. The most inexpensive option is the Polyethylene film which is normally used by gardeners for seed starting.

Greenhouse Floors

Whether you are growing your plants directly on the soil, raised beds, or in a hydroponic system, a greenhouse flooring should not only be able to serve your plants. The floor has to ensure good drainage, insulate greenhouse from the cold seeping ground, and prevent weeds and pests from coming in.Since most of the floor will be used for planting area, the flooring option should be influenced by the chosen planting method.

Soil. Your greenhouse doesn't need a finished floor surface if plants are to be grown directly on the soil. Varieties and compositions of soil beds are available and the mix you will use you will largely affect the growth of your plants and the success of your greenhouse in general.

Further Note: Old soil mix should never be reused especially that this method doesn't require plants to be raised from the ground. Ground dwelling pests can easily break in and harm your plants. In such cases where there are dead plants, it should be removed immediately from the greenhouse.

Stone, Gravel, and Pavers. These floor types are ideal for potted plants. Most commercial and residential greenhouses have raised beds directly on the floor, also making stone, gravel and pavers ideal for the setup. It allows the plant root to grow deep into the soil below the grade. Beds with pavers, flagstone, and crushed gravel are also favored materials on walkways.

Concrete. When the method of planting calls for the hydroponic or aquaponic system, self-wicking beds or tables that require a leveled surface, concrete is always a good choice. Though leveled surface can also be done with gravels and stones, concrete has more advantages when it comes to convenience and maintenance. Carts can be moved around easily with the durable and even surface. Also, the concrete slab is a solid foundation that provides additional thermal mass which helps maintain the desired temperature for your greenhouse.

WATER QUALITY AND IRRIGATION

Approximately, one gallon of water mixed with nutrients is needed daily to supply each plant. It is important to determine and make an analysis of the water quality of the greenhouse irrigation as poor quality can be responsible for slow and unhealthy growth and in some cases gradual death of plants. The alkalinity, pH, and soluble salt content are the important factors in determining the suitability of water necessary for irrigating plants.

Further Note: Reconditioning reclaimed water and run-offs or recycled water before use for irrigation minimizes the risk of disease-causing organisms, soluble salts and presence of organic chemicals that may be harmful to plants. Adjustments are as follows:

Water for irrigation should have a pH between 5.0 and 7.0. Water with pH below 7.0 is termed 'Acidic' and water with pH above 7.0 is termed 'Basic'; pH 7.0 is 'Neutral'.

pH levels should be adjusted around 5.8 to 6.5 for vegetables and crops.

If the source of water is basic more than seven parts per

million, and add acids such as nitric, phosphoric and sul-
furic.

If the water is acidic, as in less than seven, and add a base.

Watering Methods

Greenhouse plants are irrigated by means of applying
water to the medium surface. It can either be through
drip tubes or tapes, by hand using a hose, overhead sprinklers, and booms. Other methods include applying water
through the bottom of the container, sub-irrigation or by
using a combination of delivery systems. Hand watering is
fine but can really be a chore especially if you are working
on a large scale and may not efficiently saturate the media
to maintain the plant until next irrigation. Depending on
the type and size of your greenhouse, a wide range of water
systems can be used.

Sprinklers or Overhead Spray. Best for big greenhouses
that tolerate wet foliage. This irrigation system is like sat-
uration of a natural rainfall. Water is distributed through
the pipe system and then sprayed into the air through
sprinklers. The water coming out are small drops which
fall to the ground. They raise the moisture level even in
unplanted areas which set these unused sections ready for
planting.

Misting and Spray System. Works well with bigger scales,
use for propagating seeds. Misting works the same as
sprinklers but sprays a finer amount of water into the soil.
The soft water pressure is ideal for watering seedlings. It
gradually hydrates and moistens seeds without disturbing
them. They are often in automatic operation which makes
the process of watering seem effortless.

Microdrop or Seep Hose System. Efficient water system scalable to any greenhouse size. Alternatively known as drip irrigation system, a microdrop allows water to drip slowly either on the soil surface or directly into the root zone of the plant. The water runs through a network of valves, pipes, tubing, and emitters that are mounted on the media surface or buried within it. The slow dripping nature of the system there is less water waste from the run off without letting the plants dry. Automatic features include releasing water at set intervals throughout the day.

Mat Irrigation. Ideal for smaller greenhouses and novice gardeners. One way to quickly and effortlessly water plants is by placing them on seed capillary mats or self-watering trays. It's basically a tray with its own water supply often coming from the reservoir. By the time you need to water it, all you must do is top up the main water reservoir and the trays ooze water out in the capillary matting. Since water supply is drawn from the damp ground, it forces plants to grow deeper roots that can harvest more nutrients from the soil. This system is great for seedlings, freshly rooted cutting and other plants that need constant moisture. Topping up reservoirs is normally done once a week, making the method one of the lowest maintenance options which are recommended for amateur growers.

The rising demand for enhancement on water irrigation gives advent to a more innovative watering system which makes the growth of plants consistent and more uniform. Passionate growers are the first one to adopt the system. Their investment allows them to have more free time while machines take care of their plants.

Automated Irrigation System. Measures the moisture of the soil and automatically turns on or off the water system, ideal for large projects. This method is automated and trigger without you having to turn anything on or off. Depending on the set requirements, it works on a timer and provides your plants with the same amount of water. Automated irrigation is useful for big greenhouses where watering manually is time-consuming and inconvenient.

Solar Powered Irrigation System. The best solution to water management with less dependence to company utilities, perfect for small greenhouses. Equipped with solar cells, the eco-friendly irrigation system doesn't require the use of electricity. It is often in the form of drip irrigation connected to a non-pressured water source that sucks through water at regular intervals throughout the day. This makes it completely self-sufficient and the future of gardening.

WATERING TIME FOR GREENHOUSE PLANTS

Since you are growing plants in an enclosed space where there is a more control on environmental factors, determining when is the right time to water should be based on the temperature of the greenhouse. For near freezing and mildly cold temperature, water early in the day so the water in the soil acts as a trap for heat and helps the area around your plants stay a bit warmer as night approaches. Meanwhile, in humid conditions, where there is a fast absorption of the moisture of the soil, you can water at least twice a day. Just refrain from watering at the end of the day because there's a tendency that they don't get dry before sundown. If the media is damp all night, plants can be more prone to fungal and bacterial diseases.

The temperature of the room largely influences the temperature of the water. Cold surroundings could largely result to cold water temperature, same with a warm or hot environment. And you don't want to shock your plants with extreme cool or too hot water which could likely damage their tissues. Plants most likely appreciate a nice 90-95 degrees Fahrenheit. In this case, water systems with adjusted temperature range are beneficial. Other several criteria to consider before watering are the planting method, moisture level of the media, the dormancy or stage of the plant and of course the type of plant you are dealing with.

Drainage Solution

The accumulation of the depleted irrigation water, as well as rainwater from the outside, are the top concerns for greenhouse operators, especially for ornamental growers. Plants can suffer from a lack of oxygen caused by much-wet soil. Also, wet floors are prone to accidents. On the other hand, rainwater from the outside can flash flood waters inside the structure if drainage is not imposed properly. Designing a proper drainage system inside and outside the structure is a must to handle proper runoff of water sources.

DRAINAGE INSIDE THE GREENHOUSE

The foundation of the floor can play a vital role in handling water accumulation. Start with six to eight-inch gravel or stone base under the floor. This foundation can give you a collection area for over watering in such cases where there no is finished surface or concrete floors laid out. As for the method of drainage, there are two primary methods widely used.

Surface Drainage. The method is accomplished by shallow ditches or open drains that discharge larger and deeper water. The excess water is then facilitated through a created slope. A slope of eight-inch per linear foot is normally the standard.

Subsurface Drainage. The method calls for the removal of water from the root zone. This is done through deep open drains or buried pipe drains with openings so water can enter through the pipe and be discharged.

For your interiors, you can put a trench drain along the sidewalls or post lines. It may cost you more but makes the installation of the floor easier and floor drainage quicker. Incorporating soil mixes that have a good water holding capacity can also be a part of drainage solutions on your planting ground.

Peat Moss. This soft, spongy and fibrous composition is added to overworked soil that lacks structure to increase its water-holding capacity,

Perlite. What appears to be like tiny foam balls often seen in a potting medium is a component of perlite. The roundish white specks aerate the soil, boosting its water retaining properties and enhancing soil drainage.

Coarse Sand. This coarse graded material is used to make soil light and airy for the same purpose of enhancing soil drainage.

Drywell and chamber constructed in the ground facilitate water accumulation for small greenhouses. In larger structures, the drains are normally connected and lead to daylight. In some areas, greenhouse operators collect water either on a vinyl liner or sump installed below to prevent fertilizer and pesticides from getting into the water table. The water stays in the area until it dries.

ROOF DRAINAGE

Designing roof drainage becomes a factor that needs to be addressed especially on larger greenhouses where there is more accumulation of water. Greenhouse gutters, downspouts, and drain pipes can be installed to handle excess water on the roof. Downspouts direct the water to lateral pipes that are connected to a larger main. You must be cautious about the spacing as large gaps could result in water flowing over the gutter and into the greenhouse. The standard spacing should be about 50 feet apart along the gutter. For larger installations, it is recommended to install a catch basin at the end of each structure.

Drainage Area Outside the Structure

Another great drainage solution is to design a piping system that collects water and directs it to a pond or a drainage area. A detention pond can prevent water from rushing into the greenhouse in case of heavy rains. At the same time, it fends off flood from its neighboring garden. The large volume of water on the pond slowly releases over several days. In addition, it allows sedimentation, organic matter, and other pollutants to settle out before water is released.

Further Note: There are laws and regulations that govern the discharge of water into another person's property. In some locations that are covered with inland wetland code, a permit is needed to discharge water into protected areas such as swamps, protected ponds, and marshes.

Environmental Control

Greenhouses can provide its operators the opportunity to have environmental control inside the room, no matter what the weather condition outside is. Having better control means you can host the widest range of plants and can support nearly any type of plants. Depending on your commitment and budget, there are lot of climate control methods as well complex systems fitted with heating, cooling and ventilation systems.

Heating the Greenhouse

Greenhouses shelter plants by trapping solar heat and circulating air to create that artificial environment that can sustain the life when the outdoor temperature is too cool. The method can come handy for 100 percent solar heated greenhouses. But in cold-climate operating greenhouses with little or no supplementary heat, operators come up with creative ways to increase energy efficiency besides orienting the greenhouse towards the sun.

Insulation. Greenhouses uses insulation methods often incorporated in glazing and floor levels as a way of increasing energy efficiency while heating cost. Double glazing, using layers of transparent plastics covers, thermal screens and base cladding the floor are among the popular options.

Cold Frame. Built low to the ground, the transparent roofed-enclosure protect plants from extreme cold emanating from the outside. The transparent top let sunlight in and prevents heat escape via convection.

Thermal Mass. In rooms where there is little exposure to sunlight, thermal mass storages are used to collect and store sun's energy through water metal-drums. The metal transfers the sun's heat into the water. The water then radiates the heat back throughout the greenhouse. Other thermal materials that can be used with the same method are plastic tubes and concretes.

Heating Systems. Heating using light fixtures such as radiant lamp suspended over plants is one way to give necessary warmth. Combined with soil heating cables under plants, they create a warm environment. A 220-volt circuit electric heater can also work as artificial heat. There are also solar heaters as well as heating fans designed specifically for greenhouses

COOLING THE GREENHOUSE

Cooling methods are normally used in humid places and height of the summer where the hot and steamy affair is too much for plants to handle. In addition, some plants require cooler atmosphere for them to grow and that's when the cooling system come in. Each cooling method has its limits and tradeoffs that one should balance and weigh down.

Shading. Where there is an intense sunlight exposure, shading can keep plants from getting burned by reducing the amount of sunlight. Shade cloths are effective in lowering temperatures by up to 10 degrees. Roll-up screens, wood aluminum, vinyl plastic shading or paint-on materials can also be used to shade plants. The tradeoff that needed to be balanced is between lowering temperatures and losing some necessary solar radiation that is being blocked.

Fans and Vents. Excessive heat is sometimes trapped in the cosseted greenhouse. A good circulation of air can be done through ventilation and fanning. Roof and side vents can create a good through -flow of air while ceiling and exhaust fans create the necessary movement to cool down overheated plants. The only drawback with fans in dry and hot places is it can over dry foliage and planting media if overused.

Evaporative Cooling. As water evaporates, it increases the moisture level in the air. Evaporative cooling uses the natural relationship between humidity, water and air temperature for that cooling effect. The amount of cooling that can be achieved through this method is dependent on how much water can be evaporated, and relatively the humidity or the amount of water already in the air. This method gives rise to the development of evaporative coolers that automatically convert hot air into the cool breeze by using the process of evaporating water. Another system that is developed through this method is the fogging system which generates small droplets of water in the range of 10-20 microns, cooling and providing a reasonable relative humidity.

Water Damping. Wetting hard surfaces can effectively cool down hot humidity. A misting system can be used to deliver a fine spray of water in air space or in walkways. But while misting have its cooling benefit, you have to bear in mind that over wetting a canopy can lead to an increase plant diseases and fruit damage.

Further Note: You can easily feel if the indoor temperature of the greenhouse is hot or cold enough for plants to survive. However, in certain conditions, you cannot always rely on your gut feeling. Through thermometer and other climate-measuring tools, you can monitor an accurate heat or cold temperature of your greenhouse to ensure the optimal growing conditions for your plants.

PLANT POLLINATION IN THE GREENHOUSE

Birds, bees, and butterflies are some of nature's pollinators. The same barrier that protects plants from adverse growing conditions can also prevent the pollinators from doing their job. So how does pollination happen inside the enclosed structure? A little intervention can ensure that plants can be successfully pollinated even in protected greenhouses.

Manual Pollination. It may take a little of your time, but gently tapping flowers releases pollen. Disturbing flowers from male to female plants distribute pollen with each bloom.

Device Pollination. If you can't fit manual pollination into your schedule, you can use battery-operated pollinating tools. It still needs you as an operator but these tools speed up the task.

Bee Pollination. Bees by nature, are perfect pollinators. Certain bumble bee pollinators can be raised for pollination purposes. You can purchase a box or hive of bees and place in your greenhouse, as long as you also provide the supplemental food source for these pollinators.

Further Note: In a high humid environment, use fans to dry plants before pollinating them. High humidity level can cause pollen to stick together in clumps making pollination efforts unsuccessful. Also, it is best to pollinate plants between 10 am – 3 pm.

Ensuring a Pest and Disease-Free Environment

Good plant health and environmental control is your first line of defense against pests and diseases that bother your greenhouse plants. But in some instances, aphids, whiteflies, and mites can be difficult to control because of their resistance to most pesticides. However, you can still prevent and eliminate pests from lingering throughout by taking the following preventive measures and actions.

At the first sign of trouble, mechanical controls such as vacuuming, squashing and washing is necessary for biological control.

It's best to use soap or pepper sprays if pests continue to grow and multiply.

Yellow sticky traps are also effective against whiteflies.

Neem and horticultural oils manage early stages of growth of pests while pyrethroid can kill adult pests.

Meanwhile, fungal diseases are usually the greatest disease problems for greenhouse plants. The same humid temperature that favors many plants can promote these diseases, which is another reason to provide adequate ventilation system. The spacing between plants and monitoring and balancing humidity levels are ways to prevent fungal problems. In such cases where the disease already affected the plants, apply preventive sprays to minimize the affected area and isolate or quarantine the plant. If problems continue to occur, it's best to dispose of the sick plants as fungi feed more on decomposing organisms.

SAFETY AND COMFORT

Safety is one of the major concern in the greenhouse especially when it comes to electricity. Electrical shock is more likely to happen in greenhouses especially with water splashing around wherever you find plants. Avoid wetting heaters and other electrical cables. A safety check should be carried out regularly plus special care should be taken when dealing with electricity to prevent any possible contact between water and electrical connections.

As for flammable materials and gas-powered equipment, placed them far away from the heater. It is a good idea to place smoke detectors and fire extinguisher in case fire breaks in. Proper safety is also paramount to regular working activities. Sometimes, work-related injuries can be up to your own diligence but it is also dependent on a proper maintenance. Necessary repair works, whether on equipment, interiors or materials should be fixed immediately to avoid accidents.

On the other hand, comfort is also necessary to fully carry out well-tended plants and other work necessary for a productive greenhouse. For example, an easier access to the greenhouse can make it better kept especially when maintenance issues arise. Comfort also comes into play if you mix gardening with leisure space. Some incorporate a mini "living space" where they can just sit and relax while observing their plants or reading their favorite books. But whatever you envision your greenhouse will be, both safety and comfort should be considered to carry out that commitment your greenhouse need.

Budget Plans

After studying the several considerations needed to take in planning a greenhouse, you are all set to budgeting. If money is not a problem, allocating budget won't be too much of a task. In such cases where one is tight on budget, carefully allocating and dividing expenses among the materials, construction labor is a time well spent. But even though you all have that money to spare, it still wise to get some tips and money saving methods in constructing and maintaining your greenhouse. The trick is to allocate budget on the basic necessities first before going on that 'extra stuff'. Your budget will determine what you can do and put in the greenhouse. The following are the factors that needed to be on your cost accounting list. In addition, we also laid out their respective approximate cost for you to have an idea and better budget allocation.

GREENHOUSE SIZE

The larger the greenhouse, the more material it needed. It is necessary to consider how large you want your greenhouse to be if you want to avoid costly expansions.

Basic Beginner (Cost: Approximately $240). Fairly inexpensive, a 6'x8' hoop structure and greenhouse kits have everything you need to get started. Plumbing and electronics are not included in the estimation. This is an ideal setup for moderate climates.

Experienced Growers (Cost: $3,500-$7,000). A 12'x12' greenhouse with the covering of normal glass with a vented roof is recommended for more dedicated growers. Many extra costs involved laying the foundation, running plumbing and electrical system.

Serious Growers (Cost: $12,000-$25,000). A 500 to 1000-square-foot is the size for an average greenhouse structure that usually has all of the amenities including automatic watering system, feeders, and grows light. Flooring is often of poured concrete with drainage system

MATERIAL OPTIONS

The materials that will go into your design will have the biggest impact on your budget. Quality materials are often costly that's why people tend to shy away from it. It's good to have a bargain but make sure you are not skimping on the quality needed for that sturdy greenhouse construction.

Covering Materials:

Glass – about $2.50 sq.ft.

Polyethylene – about $0.12 per square foot

Fiberglass – about $72.00 per 6×8 panel

Polycarbonate – about $55.00 per 8×4 sheet

Framing Materials:

Wood, Cedar– about $1.00 per linear foot

Steel -about $2.50 per linear foot

Excavation:

Concrete – about $10.00 per square foot with texturing and drainage

Pavers – about $8.00 to $11.00 per square foot on average

Gravel – about $0.75 to $3.00 per square foot

Construction Labor Cost

Installing Lighting, Heating Ventilation and Air Conditioning (HVAC) won't be a problem with smaller greenhouses with a simple setup. For bigger projects, it will be hard even for seasoned professional to work alone, not only with these installments but with handling other construction needs. For this reason, you will need to contact licensed contractors to request a bid or quote for the work. Hiring these contractors can make up half to more than your project's total cost.

OPERATING COST AND MAINTENANCE

The expenses don't stop after the construction of the greenhouse. Operating costs involve the expenses to be paid in the plant production such seeds, substrate, pesticides and supplementary plant nutrients. Another primary cost is the utility bills such HVAC and irrigation system. Prior to investing in the construction, it is wise to examine electricity cost in your region. Evaluating the functioning expenses is necessary to determine if you can commit to the operation of a greenhouse.

Building and Zoning Permit

Some large greenhouse installations such as foundations, HVAC, irrigation, and drainage system may require installation permit and has to be done by licensed persons (as mentioned previously). In addition, 'outbuilding' or 'farm building' greenhouses may require building and zoning permit prior to the construction. It is recommended to consult your local code enforcement officer if the greenhouse you are planning to build fall under the classifications. The purpose of these permits is to evaluate if the greenhouse is a safe place for its owners and operators.

Zoning Permit. If your community is under a zoning code, the officials might require you to illustrate a greenhouse plan that shows the location of the greenhouse with relation to property boundaries and other neighboring structures. This could be the side, rear, or front lines and will be determined by your community's rules and regulations. Regulations also include accessories and the size of the building under this permit.

Building Permit. In some cases, after the zoning requirements have been met, one may be required to get a building permit. This permit is typically issued by a county department office. The code addresses structural integrity and the physical appearance of your greenhouse.

BUILDING A GREENHOUSE

Choose the Greenhouse Style / Frame

At Rimol Greenhouse Systems, we offer a variety of different styles and sizes of greenhouse structures to meet your needs. This step is one of the most critical steps in the building a greenhouse, and can determine the functionality and effectiveness of your entire operation. Each greenhouse structure is specially designed for certain applications and is best utilized in different ways. Study the description of each type of greenhouse in our greenhouse series pages to decide which structure and package will best meet your needs and budget, and use our guide to selecting a greenhouse to make your final decision. If you have further questions, or cannot decide what type of structure you would like, call us and our greenhouse technicians will assist you in planning your greenhouse project.

Step 2: Doors and Hardware

When looking at how to build a greenhouse, your Rimol greenhouse structure needs entry and exit ways that are both functional and fits with the specific look that you are trying to achieve. With our many door options in a variety of different colors and sizes, you are sure to find precisely what you are looking for. Our quality doors are guaranteed to last you a long time, and are well-insulated so heat cannot escape the greenhouse. These doors will be exactly what you need to easily access to your greenhouse at all times.

Selecting the hardware that holds your structure together is another critical step in building a greenhouse. You must be sure that your greenhouse plans include the proper nuts, bolts, and brackets so your structure will be as strong as possible under even the harshest weather conditions. Support your greenhouse with all kinds of hardware from Rimol Greenhouse Systems.

Step 3: Choose Your Covering

Choosing the proper covering is a key step in creating an effective growing environment in your greenhouse structure. Rimol Greenhouses offers a variety of coverings in different materials and thicknesses to ensure that you have options to select the exact covering that fits your needs and budget. These coverings are strong and durable, and will not tear under harsh weather conditions such as snow and wind. You can count on coverings from Rimol Greenhouse Systems to protect your greenhouse structure and last you a long time. Once you have selected your covering, be sure to read our guides on installing a greenhouse covering and installing polycarbonate.

4: Cooling and Ventilation

A common question when people ask how to build a greenhouse concerns greenhouse ventilation. It's imperative that you include a way to cool your greenhouse structure to keep plants from overheating. Rimol Greenhouses offers a variety of cooling systems, including options for mechanical ventilation, natural ventilation, and shading. Any way that you want to cool your greenhouse, we have a number of quality products that will do exactly what you need in an effective and efficient way. Take a look at our greenhouse building options for cooling and ventilation and determine the system best for you. To select what size cooling system you will need for your greenhouse structure, read through our guide on sizing fans and shutters.

Step 5: Select Your Heating System

Your greenhouse plans should also include proper heating for giving your plants a suitable growing environment. We offer heating options for every type of grower, including propane and natural gas heaters, oil heaters, convection tubing, hot water heaters and more. We can provide you with the materials for any greenhouse heating application that you would like. Browse through our selection of heating systems to decide which heating unit is right for your greenhouse structure, and then choose which size you need by using our guide explaining how to size a heating system.

Step 6: Environmental Controls

In order to create a functional and energy-efficient greenhouse structure, it is essential that you maintain complete control over the heating and cooling. From simple thermostat systems to more advanced computer modules, we have a wide range of environmental control options for every type of grower. These controls are easy to understand and extremely user-friendly, so you never become frustrated or confused. You can depend on our systems to provide you with the service you need in order to create a proper growing environment in your greenhouse. To learn more about the benefits and features of an environmental control system, read our article about understanding environmental controls.

Step 7: Other Systems

Novices looking into how to build a greenhouse should research all the systems that go into creating a fully functional greenhouse structure. A CO2 Generator can contribute to improved growth for your plants. Installing a simple irrigation system can ensure that your plants stay properly watered at all times. There are many different systems available to help you create a thriving and efficient growing environment in a controlled setting.

Step 8: Benching

When using your greenhouse structure for retail applications, benches are an essential part of making it function in ways suited for you. Our benches come in a variety of materials, styles and sizes, so that you can choose exactly which benches you would like. Made of strong, galvanized steel, these benches are sure to last you a long time. We can make virtually any custom bench, so call us and we will help you design the benches that you would like.

Step 9: Order Your Greenhouse

Once you have finalized your greenhouse plans, as well as any additional accessories, it is time to order your greenhouse structure. Fill out one of our quote request forms, and read through our terms and conditions to be sure that you fully understand the ordering process. Once you send us your order, we will have it shipped directly to you as soon as possible.

RIDICULOUSLY PROFITABLE SPECIALTY PLANTS TO GROW IN YOUR GREENHOUSE

1. GINSENG

Used for thousands of years in Asian cultures as a healing herb and tonic, this plant brings in so much profit for growers it has been dubbed "green gold". Even George Washington saw the potential of this plant; ginseng profits helped finance the Revolutionary war against the British. If you have a small vacant plot and a touch of patience this plant can reap huge rewards. Why patience? Because growing ginseng can take up to six years, as you will have to wait until the roots have fully-matured to harvest them for consumption. If that is well-beyond your time-frame, you can also sell young "rootlets" to other growers to bring some return on investment within a manageable time-frame. Over the six year period, growers can make as much as $100,000 on a half-acre plot from seeds, rootlets and mature roots. With ginseng, early birds most definitely do not get the worm.

2. GOURMET MUSHROOMS

The fungus among us grow practically anywhere in the right conditions. They also yield an incredibly high return per square foot. The two most popular gourmet mushroom varieties are oyster and shiitake, which are usually available fresh or dried in most grocery stores and Farmer's Markets. Of the two options, oysters are especially productive. They can produce up to 25 pounds per square foot of growing space area each year. When selling direct to the consumer, such as restaurants or at Farmer's Markets, oysters can bring in $7 per pound. That means a 10 x 10 square foot patch of mushrooms can bring in $17,500 per season.

3. BAMBOO

Unlike trees and many shrubs, this plant matures quickly and can bring in huge profits for growers. And maturing fast is an understatement; bamboo has been known to grow over two feet in one 24 hour period. So if you decide to go with this plant, make sure you know what you're signing up for. Bamboo is growing in popularity as a landscaping plant, and growers say their product is only increasing in demand each year. You may assume bamboo only grows in tropical climates, but these towering plants also thrive in hardy, sub-freezing weather. While the culinary uses of this plant are limited, landscapers are increasingly using bamboo as a hedge, screen, or shade plant. Many bamboo nurseries are reporting solid sales of potted bamboo at prices up to $200 per plant.

4. HERBS

Growers can prosper from incorporating herbs into their garden. Considering many herbs can grow on windowsills with limited light during winter months, this bodes well for growers looking to incorporate a plant that doesn't require excessively demanding attention. The herbs in highest demand are fresh culinary herbs for grocery stores and restaurants. Farmer's Markets are once again an excellent place to offer these plants. One way to offer them is as a 4-herb windowsill size garden that is purchased ready-to-snip. Growers may also snip and package themselves – dried or undried – for patrons looking for instant enjoyment. There's nearly no end to the choices of herb to grow, including a broad range of ethnic herbs for serious cooks. For beginnings, here's a list of the top 10 most profitable herbs you can grow.

5. MEDICINAL MARIJUANA

For growers with capital to invest upfront, medicinal marijuana (or legally-grown in Washington and Colorado) can be as profitable as Apple stores. That's right, as profitable as the most profitable company in history. Apple made about $4,650 in sales per square foot in 2013, and a dispensary in New York state could net anywhere from $3,500 to $5,000 in revenue per square foot that same year. As more states follow in the footsteps of Washington and Colorado, and the taxation for this crop is figured out on a state-by-state basis the market price may diminish slightly. But make no mistake, a 2014 article from Fast Company found that marijuana is the world's most lucrative cash crop. For those ahead of the curve (now!), the potential income from this controversial plant is immense.

ALEX PAUL M.D

Gardening is certainly not all about making money, but it's sure is nice to do once in a while. Whether you're looking to start a new business, add to your current offerings, or just generate some additional cash-flow, these five options can bring big returns for savvy gardeners. Looking for the perfect greenhouse to start this process early and grow deeper into the season? Rimol has the setup for growers of all experience levels and needs

WINDOW-MOUNTED GREENHOUSE:

These specialty greenhouses are mini and entirely economical. They are compact, small, and can fit outside the window of a house. They can either be attached to the window in such a way that access is possible from either side, inside or out. Whether used in place of the window itself or simply attached to the outside of the wall. Typically they contain about three or four shelves and extend only about a foot or more away from the wall. These types of greenhouses are most effective on a south or east facing wall and its temperature depends a lot on the interior temperature of the home or building it's attached too.

Freestanding Greenhouse:

These greenhouses tend to be the largest and most common. They are an entirely separate structure from any other building on the property and can house a large number of plants and gardening tools. These greenhouses are more easily managed despite their size beings as smaller ones tend to fluctuate temperature more often. Many sizes can be used for these greenhouses depending on the number of plants being grown and the number of gardening tools being stored.

Glazed Freestanding Greenhouse:

These greenhouses are essentially the same as a freestanding greenhouse, except they're usually made strictly of plastic sheeting. These are the least expensive of all the options, yet still, provide a large growing space for plants. The only downside of these is they tend to deteriorate more quickly and require regular upkeep throughout seasonal changes and inclement weather. However, they're considerably lightweight and retain the necessary heat for plant growth.

Any of these options make for excellent greenhouse gardening and can provide a wealth of strong, healthy plants all year round. Build your structure using strong, dependable materials such as untreated wood or aluminum. Covering options for your greenhouse frame could be made using glass, fiberglass, acrylic, polycarbonate, or even plastic (though this may need to be replaced within three years or less).

As for where to build your greenhouse, try to find a level area with adequate drainage and maximum exposure to the sun. If possible somewhere with about 6 hours of direct sunlight a day, especially during winter. If you're in an area without enough sun, special grow lights can be used to compensate, or orient the building east to west so the largest side gets full southern sun exposure.

GREENHOUSE GARDENING GUIDE

greenhouse is simply a building in which plants are grown. These buildings can be merely small structures, or they can also be quite large in size. The concept behind greenhouses dates back all the way to Roman times when the Emperor Tiberius demanded to eat an Armenian cucumber every day, for which his gardeners had to use a system similar to that in modern greenhouses to make sure he had one each day.

13th-century Italy was the site of the first modern greenhouses. Initially, greenhouses were more common on the grounds of the wealthy, but they soon also branched out to universities. The 19th century saw some of the largest greenhouses ever built, while the 20th century popularized the geodesic dome for use in many greenhouses.

Constructing a Greenhouse

Managing Greenhouses

Walnut Street Greenhouse History

Tomatoes in a Greenhouse

History of Greenhouses used for Research

ALEX PAUL M.D

Martian Greenhouses

Greenhouses in Gaza

How Does It Work? The greenhouse effect as it relates to actual greenhouses works in the following way. A greenhouse reduces the rate at which thermal energy flows out of its structure, and it does this by impeding heat that has been absorbed from leaving its confines through convection. The material for greenhouse construction is typically glass or plastic so that sunlight can pass through it. This sunlight is integral to the greenhouse becoming warm, since it heats up the ground inside the greenhouse. In turn, the warm ground then warms up the air in the greenhouse, which keeps on heating the plants inside since it is confined within the structure of the greenhouse.

GREENHOUSE USES

The purpose of a greenhouse is to shield crops from excess cold or heat and unwanted pests. A greenhouse makes it possible to grow certain types of crops year round, and fruits, tobacco plants, vegetables, and flowers are what a greenhouse most commonly grows. High-altitude countries are where greenhouses are most common; this has to do with concerns related to maintaining a viable food supply. For example, Almeria, Spain, is the site of one of the biggest greenhouses on the planet, where it is spread out over 50,000 acres.

Greenhouse Garden Gardening is one of the country's most popular hobbies, so operating a greenhouse garden is just a logical extension. A greenhouse garden is primarily meant to extend the growing season of prized crops and plants. Horticulture fans should be enthusiastic about greenhouses, too, because it allows them to grow plants and flowers all season long, which can then be brought into the house. A greenhouse garden can be built cheaply or expensively, with plastic or glass, and look attractive or simply utilitarian. After choosing a great location for a greenhouse garden, you can build one yourself by ordering a greenhouse kit from any number of popular manufacturers. These kits are do-it-yourself projects and can be as complicated or simple, or as large or small, as is desired.

Growing your own produce in a greenhouse is an incredibly fulfilling and enjoyable pass time, but as with any hobby that requires a degree of skill and knowledge, the learning curve can be quite steep. Even when growing the hardiest of plant species, there is a large number of variables that can affect growth rates and the success of a yield.

For those new to greenhouse growing, it can be hard to get everything right in your first season, and while trial and error is an important part of the learning process, these 6 tips will give any greenhouse novices a head start.

1. Seasonal Starting Seeds

One of the biggest advantages of having a greenhouse is that you can extend growing seasons, getting an early start on spring and summer and even growing certain vegetables all year round. Our growing guide gives you a good insight into what should be planted when, but before you even start planning your growing schedule, it is important that you load up on the vital seed starting supplies you'll need for a successful yield. At a minimum, you should invest in:

Growing Pots in a Greenhouse

Containers

Sterile soil (very important to reduce the chance of pest infestation and diseases)

Fertiliser

Water

We also recommend you invest in heat sources to help propagate seeds at the beginning of the season when temperatures are cooler. A propagation heating mat is an inexpensive and easy way to heat seed flats and encourage growth, but there are other methods such as heat cables buried in seed benches.

. Light Sources

During late Spring and Summer, any Swallow or Elite greenhouse should be getting enough natural light for the plants, but if you want to grow in late Autumn and Winter, a supplementary lighting system is a must-have if you want healthy, strong plants.

High output fluorescent lamp strips and LED grow lights are amongst the most popular lighting products because, unlike some other lighting systems they output full spectrum light, are very energy efficient and can cover a larger area.

However, if you're in a small and cheaper greenhouse, or are growing a smaller crop, a normal fluorescent strip hung 3-7 inches above the plants will often suffice.

3. Heating

Juliana Kerosene Greenhouse Heater

Heating a greenhouse in the cooler months can be quite the learning experience in and of itself! For those new to greenhouse growing we recommend using electric heaters as they are easier to install, more economical and have a wider range of applications. A small 120-volt heater will usually heat a small greenhouse just fine, although larger greenhouses will need a 240+ volt heater, controlled by a reliable, waterproof thermostat.

Gas heaters work just as well, but tend to be less economical and come with the added nuisance of sorting out proper ventilation, with both a constant supply of fresh air for combustion and a means of fume exhaustion.

For the eco-minded out there, less energy intensive forms of heating include setting up ventilation systems which use unneeded warm air from your home. Some growers with small greenhouses also use items like large rocks and other heat-absorbent materials which absorb heat during sunlight hours and slowly release it throughout the night. Even with supplementary heating sources, these methods are a good way of keeping the temperature inside the greenhouse more consistent throughout the course of a day.

4. Cooling

Even with the UK's milder climate, during the height of summer it can be hard to maintain a consistent temperature in a greenhouse. Because they are specifically designed to maintain and trap heat, cooling down a greenhouse that has become too hot is far harder than heating a greenhouse that is too cool.

Therefore consistently and regularly measuring the temperature inside the greenhouse or potting shed during the hotter months is hugely important. Measuring temperatures regularly can mean the difference between being able to regulate temperature by simply opening the greenhouse door and having to use positive cooling. If your greenhouse does regularly overheat, we recommend using evaporative air coolers, which maintain humidity.

5. Ventilating a Greenhouse

Seasonality plays a huge role in ventilating any size green-house. During the summer, convection currents created by the natural heat is more than enough to maintain good circulation. By keeping both the wall vents and the roof vents open during summer, cool air will be pulled in through the walls while hot air will escape through the roof, drawing in a constant supply of fresh air.

During winter, however, maintain air circulation and preventing the growth of mold can be more difficult. Making sure that the soil is not over watered will help a lot, but many greenhouse growers keep an oscillating fan running throughout most of the colder months.

6. Watering the Plants

One of the most common mistakes new growers make is watering plants according to a set schedule. A number of variables dictate when plants need watering, with temperature, humidity and the growth stage of the plants themselves having a huge effect on how much water is needed.

While in the middle of winter you might only need to water a seed bench every 10 days, during summer the frequency will be increased. The best way to know when to water the plants is to measure moisture in the soil, either with specific moisture metres or just by sight and feel of the soil.

WHY DO PLANTS GROW BETTER IN A GREENHOUSE?

A greenhouse is practically possible for a lot of yards. Many prefer these indoor settings because of their controlled environment. For example, the automatic timer connected to the watering system. It allows you to save time and control the environment depending on the season or time of the day.

Automatic ventilation controls the indoor airflow. It gives your greenhouse plants with a consistent supply of carbon dioxide. They require this for sugar and oxygen production. The concentrated carbon dioxide will result in bigger leaves and vigorous plant stems. It also increases its potential for early flowering and fruiting.

Greenhouses with moisture regulators keep the air humid for peak plant development. With a humid atmosphere, every plant can focus on flowering and fruiting. Plus a moist soil will be less likely to entertain pests and diseases.

Above is a picture of fresh kale vegetables. Below are

newly harvested carrots with the text in the middle: Easy to Grow Greenhouse Plants for Beginners.

Basics that can still influence plant growth even in a greenhouse

There are a few things to know that still can influence the growth of your plants. Some of them you probably know already from outside gardening.

Seeds

Planting using old seeds is possible. Although you may be wondering the odds of germinating them. Let us have a look at these three important elements that can affect your seeds' viability.

Age

All seeds are viable for at least one year and some are for two years. However, the germination percentages for out-of-date seeds will begin to drop after their first year.

Type

The variety of seeds can influence how long your seed stays alive. Seeds like corn and peppers will have a tough chance of surviving if they passed the two-year mark. Seeds like carrots and tomatoes can stay viable for as long as four years. While seeds like cucumber and lettuce are good for up to six years.

Storage

Old packets can have a greater possibility of keeping the seeds viable if stored properly. Seeds will stay alive much longer if they are stored in a cool, dark room.

Your vegetable drawer in the fridge is a smart option for storage.

Water

Overwatering or underwatering are usual causes of why seedlings have a delay in growth. It is normally followed by drooping or wilting. Some plants naturally absorb more than others. The quantity of water that is enough for a plant may be too generous for the other plant. When a seedling is developing slowly, observe your watering closely.

For greenhouse beginners, it might be tricky at first to find the right watering frequency. It stays moist for longer than in a garden but you also cannot rely on rain anymore. You can also organize your greenhouse plants according to their water needs in order to keep an overview.

pH level

A too high or too low pH level in the soil is the most basic reason that gardeners may overlook. It can slow down germination even if you do not see any visible signs. If you haven't been monitoring the pH, do it soon to see if that is the potential root cause of your difficulty! It is likely that the pH level at the roots is not fair for some of your plants. This is likely to happen even though they are in the same environment.

EASY TO GROW GREENHOUSE VEGETABLES

Vegetables are everyone's favorite to grow. Having your own organic veggie supply year-round is the greatest and greenhouses can be part of this healthy life.

Harvested several species of carrots

Carrot varieties

Carrots

Carrots are one of the most popular root crops that are so easy to plant. Plant them anytime even in the winter. No worries because it can tolerate frost. If you are worried about some challenges in growing carrots, then worry no more. Just prepare a loose, sandy, deeply-tilled, and loose soil. This will let them dive without pressure. Make sure that it is not too thick. Or you will end up with dwarfed, rounded carrots!

Sadly, no chemicals have been registered yet for the management of well-known carrot pests and diseases. The good news is that most of them are already resistant to most pests and diseases. Check the packets meticulously.

Sow disease-free seeds only. Regular working of the soil can overcome these obstacles. It is also okay to harvest earlier than expected. This can be done only when the damage happens late in maturity. Practice three-year crop rotation with non-susceptible plants. Always discard and destroy infected residue.

Carrots can take any time from 2 to 4 months to ripen. It depends on the type and growing circumstances. Some varieties may require a few more weeks. They are normally ready in about 75 days. Pulling may oftentimes end with a handful of leaves. But unfortunately, no carrots are attached. Loosen the soil first with a garden fork before reaping carrots.

Three green onions with a yellow pepper on the left side

Onions

Green onions

Green onions develop fast in a cold, coastal climate or a climate-controlled greenhouse. They are some of the simplest crops to produce and are practically maintenance-free. Onions are one of the most recommended starter plants. Perfect for amateur greenhouse gardeners. You can start the seedlings inside and then transplant them outdoors.

It can be planted either from seeds or sets. The easiest way is to start by developing them from sets. Onion sets are helpful as they thrive abundantly in every condition, even for cold greenhouses.

Just plant the bulbs in well-drained soil. Water the onions

regularly once they are set in your greenhouse. Do this especially when the weather is so hot. The best time to cease watering the plants is when they have swollen up. When the foliage becomes yellowish and dies back, you can now uproot it. Next is to dry them in the sun. What could be simpler than that?

They are tougher against pests and diseases. Sanitize your flats and containers with a 10% bleach solution before adding the soil, It will lessen the probability of disease.

A bunch of asparagus with a scissor below

Asparagus

Are you looking for veggies that will produce for 20 years? Garden asparagus is the answer to that. It is best planted from a one or two-year-old crown. Twenty asparagus crowns can produce sufficient supply for a household of four.

Asparagus hates competition. It is crucial to remove all the weeds and grasses around its surroundings. Never plant other crops in the same area.

The usual method of planting asparagus is in a trench. It should be about 12 to 14 inches under. Supplement the soil with lots of organic matter dug within the trench. Set the crowns 12 inches individually, with the shoots aiming up. You do not need to pick everything. If you chopped everything, the crown may die. Make sure to leave some spears preferably the smallest ones.

You can also grow your asparagus in deep containers if you want.

Don't get too excited about your first harvest. Do not pick too much from it for the first few years. They need to develop a stable root system and energy that they will require. This will provide a generous crop of spears the next season.

Spinach leaves in a white cup

Spinach

Spinach is a cold and hardy leafy vegetable. It is a common product that can be grown all year round. Most spinach thrives in cool weather. Pests are normally not a challenge, especially for a newbie.

They have comparable growing conditions as lettuce, but they are more nutritious. It can be eaten fresh or cooked. It has higher iron, calcium, and vitamin content than other raised veggies. It is even one of the excellent sources of vitamins.

Spinach loves full sun to light shade with well-drained soil. Prepare your soil with aged manure approximately one week before planting. The soil temperature should not increase more than 70ºF. The seedlings are hard to transplant. This is the reason why starting it indoors is not advised. Feed them only if needed. When seedlings germinate to a couple of inches, thin them from three to four inches apart. Keep the soil moistened with mulch.

You can already harvest the leaves just as soon as they are mature enough to eat. Remove only the outer leaves. Let the core leaves to become bigger. This will let the plant to continue growing. This technique will also temporarily delay bolting.

Four fresh eggplants with a garden background

Eggplants

Eggplants are also known as aubergine. These warm-weather greens need relatively warm conditions, like peppers and tomatoes. Raised beds enhanced with composted manure are an excellent thriving site for eggplants. The beds will warm the soil immediately.

Eggplant may tend to fall over once packed with ripe fruits. Make sure to stake them for about 24in tall. You may also use a cage to hold them upright. Check out some planters and raised beds with trellis.

Apply the finest potting mix to prevent diseases. Water them well after planting. Add a coat of mulch to maintain moisture and defeat annoying weeds. Remove the terminal buds for a thicker bush. This veggie is also excellent for pots and makes attractive decorative borders.

16 to 24 weeks after sowing is the perfect time to harvest when the skin is bright and unwrinkled. Don't pull the eggplant. Cut the fruit near the stem, leaving approximately an inch of it still attached.

Turnips

Turnips are cool-weather greens that belong to the mustard family. They grow quite fast. You can savor both the roots and the greens. Another amazing fact about this vegetable is that they sprout in just a few days. This root crop is very nutritious and adaptable to most areas.

Prepare a mixture of compost before sowing. Turnip seeds are scattered right into the soil. They do not transplant well. Make sure to prepare a permanent sunny spot for them. They do not require much attention. However, regular soil moisture is necessary.

To help overcome diseases, never plant turnips in the same spot. Practice crop rotation. Floating row covers will also shield your vegetables from pests. Since they mature quickly and get picked right away, infestations are not usually a difficulty in greenhouses. In the event you detect a problem, it is already time to harvest.

Within a month, you can already appreciate their fresh greens. The swelled roots can be harvested in the following month. Young turnips are so fragile. You can just peel and consume them just as you would an apple.

Fresh Green Leafy Kale

Kale is so nutritious with the highest antioxidant properties. It is an effective anti-inflammatory. It is best to use seeding trays for sowing. You'll be surprised that it is way easier than developing in a seedbed.

Practically no attention is needed because kale is one of the toughest and most disease resistant of all greens. Keep the weeds away with routine hoeing. Eliminate yellowing leaves which will emerge around the base of the plant.

They will thrive in nearly all situations, even with partial shade and sandy soils. Adequate sunlight is enough. But then again they will develop properly in part shade.

Kale is ideal for continuous cutting. It keeps on providing

fresh leaves for months. Pick the ground leaves first. The tip will continue to develop and produce fresh leaves.

Zucchini or Courgettes

Zucchinis are a healthy vegetable to start with especially for beginners. They are one of the simplest vegetables to grow. They typically generate a bountiful harvest in three to four weeks.

They love to spread out. You can also set them in large containers or growing bags if you have insufficient space. Remember that some seeds may fail if you buy a packet. It is best to plant all of them. If not, the seeds will not germinate well for another year.

If you are planning to plant several zucchinis, place them roughly two feet apart. They demand a lot of space to expand. It is better to stake them up so that they won't hang in an uncomfortable position. Water them adequately. Keep an eye out for some slugs.

Take good care of them as they thrive in your greenhouse. Healthy plants should start to shoot up quickly. You may want to move them into a larger container. Make sure to provide them the space they require.

Microgreens

Microgreens are also known as the vegetable confetti. They are times that they are mistaken with sprouts. They are a combination of edible young greens.

You can easily grow microgreens in a greenhouse or a cold frame. They love the full sun. They cannot tolerate freezing temperatures. Make sure that your greenhouse or cold frame has a little moisture and excellent ventilation. You can use heaters or heating pads to protect them from frost.

Each set of seeds in seed trays should be sufficient. This will make them grow in dense and hold each other. It's okay to water them from above at first to soak the soil. Bottom watering is advisable when they start to sprout. Check the absorption of water. This will also limit the growth of diseases and gray mold.

Use scissors when harvesting. You can already enjoy them in less than a month when they reach up to two inches high. The stems, seed leaves, and the first set of true leaves are all safe to eat.

Several pieces of ready to cook Okra with a chopping board on the top left side

Okra

Okra is also known as ladyfingers. It is best grown in a greenhouse. They can also thrive in containers on a shady patio but they will need more watering. You can choose Clemson's spineless variety for a long cropping period.

Drench the seeds for two hours in warm water before sowing. When the seedlings are big enough you can already transplant them into pots. Tweak those developing tips to promote bushiness. Fertilize them every week with high potassium compost when you notice the first blossoms.

The pods can be picked while they are immature because matured pods of common types are hard and stringy. Wear protective gloves when harvesting. This will prevent irritation from its tiny hairs.

FRESH AND READY TO SERVE SALAD GREENS

Salad greens

It is surprisingly easy to grow organic salads (lettuce, beet leaf, romaine, and more) every day of the year. If you plan to harvest salad greens all year round, you must plan on ordering at least eight or ten different seeds. Start with types that flourish in cool soil and moderately low light requirements. And as summer arrives, sow for heat-tolerant varieties.

Sow at least two seeds each week. Once they already have their first set of true leaves, you can transfer them to their own cells. Let them grow for another couple of weeks before transplanting them to your garden.

Your salad greens will grow after cutting them. Just leave about a half-inch of the plant behind. You can pick the leaves or the entire head. Lettuce may be cut off with scissors.

Easy to grow greenhouse fruits

The extra warmth of a greenhouse lets you grow your

favorite fruits all year round. Set your goals, wait for the satisfying results, and enjoy your gardening experience.

Red and green tomatoes planted inside a greenhouse

Tomatoes

It is easy to plant tomatoes outdoors and even easier in a greenhouse! Nothing beats a year-round supply of organic tomatoes. For starters, choose a variety that is immune to diseases like fusarium and verticillium.

Tomatoes are heat-loving plants that cannot stand the freezing weather. Inadequate light can lead to pale and frail plants. There are a lot of varieties to choose from. Choosing the best variety can be a tough task. Decide on the type of tomatoes you want. Consider the size of the full-grown tomatoes depending on your planned garden.

Make sure to plant your seeds in a soil that has proper drainage. The soil should be moistened but not immersed in water. The best temperature is around 70°F to 75°F. Place one seedling per pot for a strong and healthy tomato plant. Do not hesitate to thin the plant, because it has to be done. Start fertilizing once you see the second set of true leaves.

Organic tomatoes are healthier with greater levels of Lycopene. Lycopene helps to unclog obstructed arteries. It is also good for the heart. Another reward with growing your own tomatoes is the astounding diversity of size, shape, color, and flavor.

Planted green and red strawberries

Strawberries

Strawberry is one of the most common greenhouse fruits in the country. Greenhouse-grown strawberries taste better than those bought from a supermarket. Planting them inside a greenhouse also lessen pest and disease damage. You may also want to bring bumblebees into your greenhouse for better pollination. You can also use VegiBee garden rechargeable pollinator. Make sure to buy disease-free seedlings from reliable nursery stores. Growing strawberries doesn't have to involve so many activities. Just make sure to follow the easy steps on growing it.

Plant strawberries in pots packed with soil high in organic material. They need well-draining soil. Mulch to control the soil temperature. Drip irrigation is necessary because they have shallow roots. Sprinkling them from above may result from pests and diseases.

Make sure to keep a healthy and clean greenhouse all the time. Be alert for any indications of pests and diseases to prevent difficulties from worsening. Strawberries are also prone to verticillium wilt. You can stop this from happening by buying varieties in accredited stores. Put them away from other plants especially tomatoes

Raspberries

Raspberries can be grown in a greenhouse at any time of the year. They are easy to grow and can produce fruit regularly. Primocane bears flowers and fruits in the same year. They are capable of fruiting in their very first year of maturity. Floricanes have stems that develop for a year before producing fruit and flowers. They are usually the summer fruiting types.

They don't need additional lights and they develop properly in nearly cool conditions. A greenhouse temperature of 70°F is excellent for growth. Buy raspberry canes from a reliable garden supplier. Install a drip irrigation system for potted raspberries because overhead watering can cause rot.

The harvest season lasts between 8 and 10 weeks. Don't keep them for long. You may try freezing some for later use. Scatter them on a tray and place them in the freezer. Transfer them into freezer bags once frozen.

Cucumbers

Is the cucumber a fruit or a vegetable? It is a little bit tricky, right? But based on science, it is a fruit.

Planting cucumbers can be a bumper crop in your greenhouse. Be sure you propagate cucumbers in peat pots, not in flats. Their cucurbit root systems must not be obstructed.

There are a couple of ways for training vines when raising in a greenhouse. First is the triple stem training method. All suckers are taken off the developing creeper up to the head of the trellis. The other approach is the lateral growth training. Each sucker is pinched off for the first 4 to 5 fruit sets.

A few pests and diseases might risk your cucumbers' growth. The spider mites are microscopic. You will see them webbing the stem and leaf. Insecticidal soap can help reduce their populations.

Cucumbers grow fast. Never let them become too big because it will taste bitter. Harvest every two days. Keep picking. Because they will stop producing as they mature.

Several pieces of red and yellow peppers

Bell peppers

Have fun gardening with easy to grow pepper varieties. Peppers are colorful plants. The variety of shapes and sizes is one of the best aspects of your greenhouse. The distinct flavors varying from light and sweet to eye-watering spicy. It is something to satisfy everyone's taste among different varieties ready from seeds.

Peppers need a fairly long growing period to give the best results of sweetness or spiciness. Pack your seed tray and water the soil with fertilizer before scattering your seeds on its surface. Once they are well-established, the roots will begin to stretch in the cells. This is the right time to transplant them into pots. They don't expect pinching or training. When they start to flower, the stems will manage to branch out naturally.

Always watch for colonies of aphids on leaves. They suck the sap and secrete sticky honeydew. This will promote the increase of black molds. Use your fingers to squish these colonies or apply biological control. Dark spots may develop on the ends. Water regularly and not intermittently. Do not let your soil dry out.

Harvest peppers as soon as they reach the right size. Fully grown peppers are the most nutritious and tastiest. Picking them regularly will stimulate more fruits. It is better to use a sharp knife or scissors so that they won't be easily damaged when cutting it.

CHERRIES

Cherries are one of those fruits that can be planted in a greenhouse. Potted cherries take up smaller greenhouse place and are movable. Cherry species that do not need cross-pollination are one of the easiest to grow.

They would fruit as they would outdoors with the right combination of soil, temperature, water, and nutrients. Fertilize your cherry trees once a year. Be sure your greenhouse is well ventilated. Keep the temperature from rising quickly especially in summer. Prune it lightly using scissors. Remove every broken or dead branch. Prevent diseases by implementing good airflow, pruning, and thorough cleaning. Do not leave the leaves or aged fruits on the ground.

We know that you are excited to harvest your cherries but you need a lot of patience. Harvesting them too soon may result in ruining your fruit. It will take up to 3 years to produce proper fruits.

Cantaloupe melon

Cantaloupe

Growing cantaloupe or muskmelon in a greenhouse is so satisfying. The answer is lots of moisture, sunshine, and warmth. If you have a small space, its vines can be trained using a trellis. They love loamy and well-drained soil. They also need pollination to produce fruit. Bees can help!

Thinning lessens the competition for space, nutrients, and water, to provide healthy growth. Companion planting is one of your best defense from pests. Try planting dill to ward off these bugs. Inspect your vines at least twice a week.

A crack in the stem where the fruit is attached is a sign that your melon is already ripe. This sun-ripened fruit is packed with antioxidants and vitamin C into every bite. It perfectly blends great flavor with great nourishment.

Vine

Grapes

You are right! You don't need a vineyard to grow your own yummy grapes. They are not really as demanding to grow as they seem. It only takes a little attention to watering, training, fertilizing, and pruning. It is achievable to pro-duce a stable crop year after year.

Greenhouse vines need to be planted at the opposite edge to the door. Then the stems trained on the side of the greenhouse alongside the ridge of the roof and moving close to the door. For bigger greenhouses, you can start it with the root outside, or inside. Water them every 7 to 10 days throughout the growing period.

Greenhouse grapes may need a little help with pollination when the vine develops into flower. Remove these curly tendrils as they appear. They will just get tangled up with the fruits. Leave the vines scrambled rather than adhering to your pruning and training course.

You can even increase your possibilities of getting a good harvest. One vine is enough to grow in a tub for small greenhouses.

Chilies

Chilies may seem like a veggie but it is surprisingly not. They are clearly a fruit. The secret to an abundant harvest of chilies is a long and hot growing period. This is the reason why they are famously nurtured in a greenhouse.

The germination is normally from a week to 10 days. Pick the main stalk when it reaches about 11 to 15 inches high to promote a lot of side shoots to progress. They love water but make sure not to drown them. There are times that whiteflies may bother them. They are normally caught from another plant like tomatoes. Use yellow sticky cards to manage minor infestations.

Use scissors or a sharpened knife to pick green or red chilies. However, some variations of chilies will not go red in certain environments. You can harvest them green and they will turn red. But they will appear wrinkled and dry out. It is better to leave them on the plant until needed.

Lemons

Lemons are pretty simple to grow considering they need little attention once planted. It will thrive if the moisture, lighting and temperature conditions have adhered. Think of the dwarf varieties that are well-suited to containers. This allows a lot of gardeners everywhere to appreciate the privileges of homegrown lemon trees.

Lemon trees grow best in an inside a temperature-controlled greenhouse where it stays between 70°F to 90°F. Lemon trees need at least eight hours a day of sun to grow. But if you can provide 12, that will be best! They absolutely require intense daylight to induce flowers and have the energy to bear fruits.

Conduct a taste-test to decide if the fruit is sweet enough because skin color doesn't mean ripeness. Lemons may be picked over several months. The conventional storage advice is to leave them on the tree until you are willing to consume it.

EASY TO GROW GREENHOUSE HERBS & SPICES

Medicinal and culinary herbs can now be within your reach on a daily basis. These recommended easy to grow herbs are guaranteed to jumpstart your gardening hobby.

A mint tea with mint leaves

Peppermint

Mint

The lively and invasive characteristics of mint make it relatively easy to grow. Mint carries out lateral root runners beneath the soil. It will also appear in other parts of your area. They compete with other plants for water, light, and nutrients at the same time.

Plant mint for about 2 inches under and 12 inches apart. Water it well. Measure the roots' tendency to reach nearby plant roots by settling boards. You can put bricks one foot deep throughout beds. You may also place it a big deep plastic canister sunken into your garden bed. You can also simply use a pot or container and place it above the ground or on a shelf.

If you notice some signs of mint rust then eliminate and destroy it. They can quickly spread to other plants and soil. It will soon affect new crops in the future.

You can brew mint leaves into tea, or garnish chilled drinks. Spearmint is commonly used to create mint flavoring or jelly. Try sprinkling dried or raw leaves over plain lamb before cooking. Savor that distinctive taste!

Cilantro

Cilantro thrives in pots and well-prepared gardens with loose, well-draining soil. This herb can reach up to 3 feet in height. They are easy to grow and will self-seed.

This herb needs consistent watering. They do well in full sun and loose soil improved with organic materials. They will flower and go to seed soon in warm conditions. Do not transplant them. The long taproot is so fragile and if injured, the herb will fail to grow. The seeds sprout at temperatures ranging from 50°F to 85°F. It will usually occur in 7 to 10 days.

Discard those dead leaves and pick up debris on the ground. Wash the leaves from time to time to disturb the regular spore-releasing cycle. Neem oil and PM wash applied on a 7-day schedule can stop a fungal invasion. Apply a slow-release organic compost. Never apply unnecessary nitrogen.

Harvest fresh leaves as needed. Cilantro is best harvested early in the morning. Don't wash the leaves because the fragrant oils will be lost.

Sage

Sage can be grown from seeds easily. We suggest starting this hardy perennial with other herbs, like rosemary, and basil. You can set out greenhouse-grown seedlings approximately one foot apart.

Spider mites and slugs are a few of the typical pests seen on sage. Eliminate weeds and other garden trash. Discard seriously infested plants by placing them in the trash.

Harvest the leaves delicately throughout the first year of growth. Pick as needed in the coming years. Sage is best consumed fresh but can also be stored. Dried leaves have a powerful and somewhat different taste than the fresh one.

Dried sage leaves are a traditional ingredient for turkey stuffing. The seeds are ready to collect when the blossoms become brown and dry. When it is fully dry, lightly crush the heads and carefully extract away the waste.

Planted Tarragon herb with flowers

Tarragon

Tarragon is best developed from seedlings, cuttings, and seeds. It is normally easier to plant about 4 to 6 seeds each pot. Apply moistened and composted potting mix. These herbs need to be raised in areas that can get full sun. Ensure adequate airflow.

These hardy herbs can tolerate and even grow in areas having poor, dry, and sandy soil. Tarragon has a strong root system. It makes them quite tolerant of desert conditions. They will survive for 2 to 3 years. However, they will finally run out of steam and need renewing.

There are two varieties of tarragon. First is the French tarragon, which is fully flavored and fancied by foodies. Then the Russian tarragon, which has less flavor.

Set out greenhouse-grown tarragon 18 inches apart. You can cut both the flowers and leaves.

Thyme herbs that are starting to blossom

Thyme

Thymes are easy to grow from seed. The germination period may take some time (from 14 to 28 days). Seedings are best started indoors where the temperature can be maintained at around 70°F. Therefore, a greenhouse is the perfect place for it.

Sow seeds in superficial rows about one foot apart. When your seedlings are stabilized, thin them to 6 inches apart.

Harvest thyme before their flowers starts to open. Cut the herb with 1.5 to 2 inches from the spot. A second growth will emerge but this must not be cut. This would lessen the plant's winter hardiness. Although it is a hardy perennial, they still need a little bit of attention over the winter months to withstand the cold environment.

Bay leaves

Bay laurel is an evergreen plant or tree. It is the easiest herb to grow in a greenhouse. It can even survive drought. This tender perennial grows between 3 to 5 feet and even up to 15 feet in tropical climates. Its shiny, durable leaves have many culinary values. Bay laurel is best raised in a container. Random pruning will keep the desired appearance.

Bay laurel leaves can be picked during the season as required. The bigger and older leaves have the strongest flavor. Dry the leaves before saving in sealed packages. This herb can be saved for up to one year. It is a bonus to have at least one bay laurel tree in the corner.

Catnip

Catnip generates quickly from both seeds and leaf-tip cuttings. This perennial herb grows up to 3 feet and it loves full sunlight. It has grey and green leaves with violet blossoms. It easily grows in sunny spots, with enough space, and regular water with excellent drainage. If it goes into flower, cut off the buds to promote stronger and healthier leaf growth.

Be cautious not to excessively mist your plant to control mold growth. Protect them with an arched-shaped wire mesh. This technique will prevent any interested cats in rubbing and licking the herb and will not harm the plant itself.

Catnip attracts helpful insects. You will love it in teas for recreation. Also, try to rub it on your skin. It will act as a natural insect repellant. This is useful to use as a companion plant to repel bugs. Both you and your cat can enjoy the benefits of having catnip grown nearby.

ROSEMARY

Rosemary is an evergreen woody herb. They grow slowly in their first year or two. It will increase up to 4 feet high with an extent of 6 to 8 feet, depending on your preferred type.

There are two main types of rosemary. The upright and the creeping. Both of them are extremely fragrant. Uprights are completely suited for shaping and as individual plants. The creepers, on the other hand, are good for ground coverings or added slope resistance. Greenhouse coverings can also help you deal with annoying weeds.

It can become sensitive to powdery mildew when packed or planted in wet places. Make sure they have lots of sunlight and adequate airflow to restore vitality.

It is a strongly flavored herb used in cooking and as an element in bouquet topping for soups. Its flowers are more delicately seasoned than its leaves. You will definitely love it on your salads.

Anise

Anise is so easy to plant. It prefers full daylight and well-drained soil. You can instantly sow seeds or cuttings in your greenhouse.

Anise is a little annual herb with white or faint yellow blossoms. Its scent is comparable to fennel, caraway, dill or licorice. It is native to the Mediterranean and Southern Europe. You can also see them growing wild in open lands.

This plant has lacy leaves and peaks of white blossoms. It gives way to seeds bearing savory oils that taste so great! When blossoming, it presents an abundance of flowers. An anise plant grows between 18 to 24 inches tall.

Star anise thrives in places where the temperature doesn't drop under 15°F. If you reside in a cooler state below USDA Zone 9, you can plant this herb in a pot. Then you can put it inside a greenhouse in wintertime or grow it inside your greenhouse all year. Harvest the flower peaks after the seeds have grown, and when the flower head has fallen. Read more about growing anise in a greenhouse here!

Cumin

Cumin is the second most famous spice in the world! It belongs to the parsley species. It grows high and has slim dark green leaves between 6 to 24 inches high. It is usually grown from seed which you can instantly sow in your greenhouse. Cumin seeds germinate in roughly 7 to 14 days. You can speed up the process by drenching the seeds in water for about 8 hours before sowing. Plant them in containers or raised beds wherever you feel comfortable.

It has a nutty, peppery, sour taste with a rich fragrance and high oil content. Grow the plants in full daylight. It grows fine in normal, well-draining soils. Water regularly. The trick is harvesting the pods when the first ones are roughly spilling the seeds.

Remove the ripen pods and let them turn brown and dry.

Next, rub the pods to extract seeds. You can try to take the whole stem and place them upside down in a container in order to get the seeds.

Lavender

Lavender is a strong drought-resistant perennial. It is the most famous of all sweet-smelling herbs. When it blooms, the fragrance drifts pleasingly everywhere. They can become as high as 2 feet. Put the seedlings in a sunny part of the greenhouse. You may also use grow lights because it grows abundantly in full daylight.

Lavender can be forced to flower during the year. You can produce 16-hour days or a 4-hour night break. It will develop in about 8 to 10 weeks if forced in 64°F to 68°F temperatures.

Lavender may be subjected to several pests and diseases. Prevention is the best solution! Supplying good airflow and letting plants to dry somewhat between waterings will help in generating a healthy harvest. They do fine in most soils as long as it is well-drained. Harvest them early in the morning when their oils are at their strongest.

Licorice

Licorice has been loved even in biblical times ago. It was even discovered in King Tut's tomb. It is surprisingly a member of the pea species. It grows up to 5 feet tall. This herb has a flavor like Anise but they are not linked.

Licorice is a natural remedy for menstrual cramps and the pain of menopause. It is also used as a treatment for ulcers. Some people use it for breast and prostate cancer therapies. This herb is also said to be beneficial for the adrenal gland. It reduces the impact of aging on our brain. It can be used in teas, flavoring many foods, beer making, and an additive in tobacco.

They grow adequately in slightly alkaline soil. The soil must be deep and moistened. The shrubs can be started from seeds and cuttings. They grow best in the broad sun to partial shade.

Let the fresh shrubs to mature for 3 years before harvesting the roots. When harvesting, get the horizontal roots. Never take the main taproot.

Easy to grow greenhouse flowers

Grow your flowers in a greenhouse and get a spring feeling even in winter. These easy to grow flowers will surely give you the perfect ambiance. Relax and have fun gardening!

African violets

African violet is so easy to look after and will bloom over and over again even during the long winter months. They are one of the most attractive flowers. This all-time favorite blossoms on several occasions every year.

African violets love the warm environment (not more than 85°F but not less than 65°F). You can keep it flourishing in bright but indirect daylight with moistened soil. They can thrive well underneath artificial lighting if days are too short. Excellent drainage and an African violet fertilizer applied every fortnight can help.

Remember that if the soil is extremely dry or there may not be sufficient light, it may produce less to no flowers at all. Do not use cold water because it will create spots on its leaves. Read more about growing African violets in a greenhouse here!

Peace lily

The peace lily is one of the well-known houseplants. They are easy to cultivate and a pretty decoration, too! All you need is to imitate the tropical environment in your greenhouse. Peace lilies may produce white to off-white flowers. This flower will continue to bloom especially with adequate light.

Peace lilies rather tolerate underwatering than overwatering. It is one of those numerous reasons why they usually die. Easily feel the top of the soil to observe if it is already dry. If it is, then you can water your plant. If it is still moist, it doesn't require watering.

Peace lilies may rise between 1 to 6 feet high. Better check the expected height. These lilies can also purify toxins from the surroundings, according to NASA. The downside is that it may induce stomach and respiratory irritability if consumed or inhaled in large quantities. Remember to keep peace lilies away from small children and pets. Get more details about growing peace lilies in a greenhouse here!

Kalanchoe

Kalanchoe blossfeldiana is one of the most famous potted flowers in a greenhouse. The lush stem-tip cuttings are almost easy to develop. Postharvest production is great. It provides long-lasting flowers which serve as a magnificent decoration for your greenhouse or your house. They are short-day plants. It flowers when the day time is equivalent to or less than 12 hours.

A lot of flowering potted plants are grown in autumn, winter and early spring. This is when the actual light levels are weak.

This water-retaining plant produces bright, bell-shaped flowers. It also needs very little attention. Kalanchoe embraces dry environments and temperature fluctuations. It is also excellent with 45°F wintertime climate.

Begonia

Begonias are easy for any gardener to take care of. It doesn't matter whether they are set indoors or outdoors. They also appear in varying foliage colors and designs. Replant them in beautiful hanging baskets, pots or containers. You can choose from a fibrous or tuberous variety.

These flamboyant blossoms simply need some occasional watering and even less water in wintertime. It is beneficial to water first thing in the morning. This will stop water spotting or burning of the leaves on summer days.

Begonias are also susceptible to powdery mildew. It is best to regulate humidity, improve airflow, and grow with warm temperatures.

Proper heat and light will let begonias to grow full and quickly. These flowers will persevere in even the cloudiest spots in summer.

Marigold

These easy to care, brilliant flowers are oftentimes used as Mother's Day presents. They are displayed individually or in bunches. Marigold flourishes in abundant sunlight. This flower usually endures very hot seasons. They produce satisfying results in reasonably fertile, dry or well-drained ground. Marigold has few pests difficulties. Once they are grown and fixed, try pinching off the tips to boost them to become thicker. Water at the bottom of the plant.

Once flowers are planted, they will only require very little attention. Just water them regularly and don't let the soil dry out.

Sunflowers

A favorite to almost everyone. You will unquestionably be fascinated with the sunflowers stretching up to 10 feet high! Simply scatter the seeds right into the soil in a sunny, protected place and watch them blossom.

Sunflower seeds sprout quickly when originated in greenhouses before the start of the growing period. Expose these sun-loving flowers to direct daylight for at least 10 to 13 hours a day. You can also provide artificial light if natural light fails to satisfy them.

Slugs and snails love to eat fresh and developing shoots. Protect them by using a covering defense, like the head of a plastic bottle. As the sunflower takes form and begins to grow higher, you may want to hold the plant straight up. For the best outcome, tie a stick to the stem using strings.

Nigella

Nigella (love in a mist)

Nigella is an amazingly easy flower to grow. Just spread the seeds over a spot of naked soil, rake it, and let it take care of itself! They look great in planters and hanging baskets.

Their seeds love a sunshiny spot but they are also fine with a shady spot. It self-sows easily but is not annoying. You may choose to think about border edging to restrain them. It doesn't want being transplanted so it is always best if sown directly.

Amidst jewel-like blossoms and fragile ferny leaves, it is much sturdier than it seems. As the flowers wither, this attractive flower will produce seed for the next year. It is practically pest-free because they do not last long enough to be disturbed by any pests or disease.

Daisies

Most gardeners enjoy their easy to grow character. They appear to grow in all forms and sizes.

Daisies are usually developed from seeds. Healthy soil is the key to planting most flowers. The soil needs to be fertile and well-draining. Constant trimming and dead-heading are what keeps them flowering.

Daisies are rarely disturbed by pests and diseases. They generally do not require insecticides. On some isolated circumstances where pests and diseases are a difficulty, you can treat them with a bar of insecticidal soap at the initial sign of a problem.

Plant in full sun and water completely but never over water. This will make them overly tall and lanky which re-quires staking. If they are in a shady place, they will reach for the sunlight and fall over.

Morning glories

Are you looking for a fabulous, quick flowering climber that will overwhelm you with a wealth of blossoms? Why don't you give morning glories a shot? The large, perfumed flowers unfold to welcome the morning sun, then close up at lunchtime.

If you want to enhance the germination speed, immerse it in warm water for a couple of hours. Make sure you have something for them to go upward to flash their brilliance. Morning glories love the bright sunlight. They will even grow in normal to weak soils. It just a little attention so this is really great for kids and inexperienced gardeners. They are usually not even bothered by pests and diseases.

They are not safe for ingestion because most portions and seeds are toxic. Morning glories are recognized as harmful weeds to some people. It is against the law to plant them in Arizona. Read this to get more details about growing morning glories in a greenhouse!

BENEFITS OF GARDENING USING OUTDOOR STRUCTURES AND GREENHOUSES

Longer Growing Season

One of the main advantages to growing in a greenhouse is that it offers you a longer growing season.

Temperatures don't vary as much within a greenhouse, since the sun's radiation is trapped in the enclosure, retaining the heat within the structure.

Growing seasons can be extended, even in cold climates.

Garden in Any Weather

Keeping up a garden in bad weather can be difficult. With a greenhouse, you don't have to worry about this since everything is covered. Even if it's pouring rain outside, you can garden and keep dry.

Grow a Wide Variety of Plants

You have the ability to grow a wide variety of plants when using a greenhouse. It allows individuals to enjoy experimenting with exotic plants that are not found in the local area.

Protection from Pests and Predators

The production from pests and predators by the greenhouse is another huge advantage.

Pests and predators like moles, deer and squirrels can be easily kept out.

Smaller pests, like certain rodents, can be kept out with the addition of traps and screens.

Strong greenhouse plastic can be purchased from online retailers (like Simply Plastics, for example), which can make the process much easier.

Create the Optimum Growing Environment

With a greenhouse, you have the ability to create the optimum growing environment for plants, whether you're growing herbs, vegetables, flowers or other types of plants.

Creating an optimum growing environment helps you to enhance the growth of plants, giving you the benefit of healthier, better producing plants.

Protect Plants from Bad Weather

Bad weather can end up destroying plants, even in the best tended outdoor garden. Bad weather like high winds, dust storms, thunder storms and blizzards can all cause damage. However, a greenhouse offers plants a layer of protection from the elements.

Go Green with Your Greenhouse

Growing plants within a greenhouse allows gardeners to go green, which is a benefit to gardeners and the earth. Adding more plants helps to provide a fresher, cleaning atmosphere, making a greenhouse a great tool for fighting global warming.

GROW PLANTS WITHOUT DANGEROUS PESTICIDES

Many people are unhappy about the dangerous pesticides found on many commercially raised crops.

It's possible to grow plants without all those dangerous, toxic pesticides when growing in a greenhouse. Gardeners can control what they use when growing their own produce.

Keep Beneficial Insects Inside

Certain insects are beneficial to plants, such as ladybugs.

They can help to keep the population of nuisance insects under control. In an open air garden, beneficial insects can easily leave.

However, greenhouses contain these insects, which can keep problems with nuisance insects from occurring.

Easily Customize the Greenhouse to Your Needs

When you build a greenhouse, you have the ability to

easily customize it to your needs.

This means you can decide on a greenhouse that works well with the types of plants you intend to grow.

Enjoying Raising Your Own Food

Some individuals grow plants as a food source. Using a greenhouse to grow food year round allows gardeners to enjoy the advantage of lower food bills.

Save Energy

Greenhouse gardening can even offer the advantage of saving energy.

When using a greenhouse, it's possible to conserve energy sources like water, since these energy sources can more easily be controlled as opposed to traditional gardening

Using a greenhouse is not just about the benefits and advantage's of growing plants, but also about changing the lifestyle's and live a more environmentally friendly life.

It's also about teaching children and family members to garden, as it is a vital skill to learn and brings families closer together.

RELAXATION AND STRESS RELIEF

Last, growing plants within a greenhouse offers the advantages of relaxation and stress relief.

It offers a great place where you can get away and enjoy tending the plants.

Gardening can help to reduce stress levels and using a greenhouse makes sure you can enjoy this all year long.

Greenhouse Systems, we offer a variety of different styles and sizes of greenhouse structures to meet your needs. This step is one of the most critical steps in the building a greenhouse, and can determine the functionality and effectiveness of your entire operation. Each greenhouse structure is specially designed for certain applications and is best utilized in different ways. Study the description of each type of greenhouse in our greenhouse series pages to decide which structure and package will best meet your needs and budget, and use our guide to selecting a greenhouse to make your final decision. If you have further questions, or cannot decide what type of structure you would like, call us and our greenhouse technicians will assist you in planning your greenhouse project.

Doors and Hardware

When looking at how to build a greenhouse, your greenhouse structure needs entry and exit ways that are both functional and fits with the specific look that you are trying to achieve. With our many door options in a variety of different colors and sizes, you are sure to find precisely what you are looking for. Our quality doors are guaranteed to last you a long time, and are well-insulated so heat cannot escape the greenhouse. These doors will be exactly what you need to easily access to your greenhouse at all times.

Selecting the hardware that holds your structure together is another critical step in building a greenhouse. You must be sure that your greenhouse plans include the proper nuts, bolts, and brackets so your structure will be as strong as possible under even the harshest weather conditions. Support your greenhouse with all kinds of hardware Greenhouse Systems.

Choose Your Covering

Choosing the proper covering is a key step in creating an effective growing environment in your greenhouse structure. Greenhouses offers a variety of coverings in different materials and thicknesses to ensure that you have options to select the exact covering that fits your needs and budget. These coverings are strong and durable, and will not tear under harsh weather conditions such as snow and wind. You can count on coverings Greenhouse Systems to protect your greenhouse structure and last you a long time. Once you have selected your covering, be sure to read our guides on installing a greenhouse covering and installing polycarbonate.

Cooling and Ventilation

A common question when people ask how to build a greenhouse concerns greenhouse ventilation. It's imperative that you include a way to cool your greenhouse structure to keep plants from overheating. Greenhouses offers a variety of cooling systems, including options for mechanical ventilation, natural ventilation, and shading. Any way that you want to cool your greenhouse, we have a number of quality products that will do exactly what you need in an effective and efficient way. Take a look at our greenhouse building options for cooling and ventilation and determine the system best for you. To select what size cooling system you will need for your greenhouse structure, read through our guide on sizing fans and shutters.

Select Your Heating System

Your greenhouse plans should also include proper heating for giving your plants a suitable growing environment. We offer heating options for every type of grower, including propane and natural gas heaters, oil heaters, convection tubing, hot water heaters and more. We can provide you with the materials for any greenhouse heating application that you would like. Browse through our selection of heating systems to decide which heating unit is right for your greenhouse structure, and then choose which size you need by using our guide explaining how to size a heating system.

Environmental Controls

In order to create a functional and energy-efficient greenhouse structure, it is essential that you maintain complete control over the heating and cooling. From simple thermostat systems to more advanced computer modules, we have a wide range of environmental control options for every type of grower. These controls are easy to understand and extremely user-friendly, so you never become frustrated or confused. You can depend on our systems to provide you with the service you need in order to create a proper growing environment in your greenhouse. To learn more about the benefits and features of an environmental control system, read our article about understanding environmental controls.

Other Systems

Novices looking into how to build a greenhouse should research all the systems that go into creating a fully functional greenhouse structure. A CO2 Generator can contribute to improved growth for your plants. Installing a simple irrigation system can ensure that your plants stay properly watered at all times. There are many different systems available to help you create a thriving and efficient growing environment in a controlled setting.

: Benching

When using your greenhouse structure for retail applications, benches are an essential part of making it function in ways suited for you. Our benches come in a variety of materials, styles and sizes, so that you can choose exactly which benches you would like. Made of strong, galvanized steel, these benches are sure to last you a long time. We can make virtually any custom bench, so call us and we will help you design the benches that you would like.

ORDER YOUR GREENHOUSE

Once you have finalized your greenhouse plans, as well as any additional accessories, it is time to order your greenhouse structure. Fill out one of our quote request forms, and read through our terms and conditions to be sure that you fully understand the ordering process. Once you send us your order, we will have it shipped directly to you as soon as possible.

Build Your Greenhouse

Finally, after selecting all of the equipment that will make up your greenhouse, you must build the structure. While this may seem like a daunting task Greenhouse Systems has numerous instruction manuals and fact sheets that can help you construct your greenhouse without a problem

Essential Greenhouse Accessories

Greenhouse Heating

There are normally two types of heating systems when it comes to greenhouses, a central system and a unit system. Which one you need will depend on a variety of things, including what sort of plants you are planning to grow and the size of the greenhouse itself. Each heating system has unique benefits, as well as disadvantages so it is important you properly research which one would most suit your particular gardening needs.

Greenhouse Ventilation

In order to maintain a proper greenhouse environment, you should invest in a ventilation system. You can choose from an automatic or manual system. Automatic systems offer convenience because an automatic timer will open the vents of a greenhouse when a certain temperature is reached. In some cases, a fan may also be activated. Manual systems rely on a person opening them by hand and are generally good for using only in very basic greenhouses.
Plant Fertilizer

No greenhouse plants would be complete without a supply of plant fertilizer to aid healthy growth. While standard fertilizers are relatively inexpensive, the more expensive organic fertilizers are gaining in popularity. Not only are the organic options good for the plants, they help protect the surrounding environment too.

Greenhouse Pest Control

Every gardener is aware of the need to protect their plants from both walking and flying pests. Therefore, no green-house is complete without a decent pest control system. As well as the standard pesticides, there are several eco-friendly versions for those worried about inadvertently damaging their plants or the environment. A simple mesh will help to keep out flies and other small bugs.

Greenhouse Watering Systems

Water wands release tiny droplets of water in a fine mist directly over the plants. These wands work on a timer, so you will have peace of mind regarding your plant's water supply. Drip systems are often larger and supply a greater quantity of water. A drip system also uses a timer and is ideal for a large area watering.

Greenhouse Irrigation Systems

If you have an active water system you will also need to implement an irrigation system to get rid of excess and waste water from the greenhouse. Virtually all systems work in a similar fashion with only size to differentiate them. They all work by carrying excess water away from the plants and into a designated area, which is usually the soil in your garden.

Greenhouse Staging & Shelving Systems

Growing racks are great space savers for smaller green-houses. They are designed to protect plants from harsh weather conditions and accidental knocks. For smaller structures, greenhouse shelving units are often used as either a two-tier freestanding unit, three-tier freestanding unit, or a four-tier freestanding unit. These units are easy to assemble and the shelving is essential for keeping a greenhouse tidy and organized.

Lighting

Lighting units provide basic light for when you need to work in your greenhouse when there is little natural sunlight. The units should be waterproof and feature a safety trip-switch that will automatically stop the flow of electricity if the unit is compromised by bad weather, water or anything else. Greenhouse lighting is essential for winter gardening, when hours of daylight are drastically reduced.

Digital Thermometer

A thermometer may be a small accessory, but it is definitely one of the most important when it comes to greenhouse gardening. Because certain plants grow best in certain temperatures, a thermometer will help ensure the proper temperature is achieved and if the temperature drops below a safe limit. Plants do not fare well in cold weather and frost can kill them quickly, so a thermometer helps ensure your greenhouse temperature is regulated.

Greenhouse Coverings

Everyone knows that plants need sunlight to grow however, not everyone knows that too much sunlight can be detrimental to their growth. Cloth shades fit on the windows and can be pulled down when the sunlight is strong, to give the plants some shade. The shades will also help prevent the inside temperature from becoming uncomfortable.

Cleaning Kit

Special micro-fiber cloths and demister spray are essential cleaning items for a greenhouse. Used together they help eliminate condensation on greenhouse windows, which reduces the chances of mold and mildew.

GREENHOUSE TOOLS & EQUIPMENT

1. Hand Trowel

A garden trowel is stated to be the main essential gardening tool for all gardeners. Used by all gardeners, the trowel is used for planting, transplanting and potting. Designed to be handheld, the handle is usually made from rubber, plastic or metal. The shovel-like blade is made from stainless steel as overtime, tools in the garden especially hand trowels can begin to decay and damage.

2. Spade

Every serious gardener should have a spade, if not, your gardening kit isn't complete. With its long handle and narrow flat head design, digging tasks as well as edging beds, lawns, transplanting, and many more gardening activities will most definitely be a hard task without one. Again, comfort, size and material will all depend on you and your style of gardening.

3. Fork

Finding a multi-purpose gardening tool can seem like a

gardeners dream. Owning a Fork can be a dream come true, with its power to aerate lawns, break compacted soil, create holes for seeds and mix in soil treatment, are just to name a few of the tasks a fork can handle. Through it's sharp and strong fork-like figure, penetrating difficult terrain has never been so easy to do.

4. Secateurs

Secateurs, also known as pruning shears, or clippers, are used by all gardeners to enable shaping, trimming and removing of dead growth from plantations. Thick branches can also be cut and trimmed depending on the quality of the secateurs blades, remember that the grip is just as important as the head of the tool!

5. Hoe

Preparing beds for planting and weeding can in some cases be a very difficult garden task. However, with a garden hoe, cultivating your soil and edging your garden grass can be done with ease. This essential garden tool can come in several styles, Draw or Dutch. All varieties of hoe slice the top of your weeds, if used in a sweeping motion.

6. Gardening Gloves

No matter what garden tool you own, no tool is as important as your hands. Using a pair of gardening gloves prevents thorns, splinters and dirt from being in contact with your skin. Comfort and protection are the main factors when buying a good pair of gardening gloves.

7. Rake

Stones, rocks and clogs are a gardener's nightmare when planning to plant. A rake will remove these as well as levelling and smoothing out the surface of your soil. This garden essential is another multi-purpose tool as it is also used to collect leaves, weeds or any other debris. As well as the hoe, multiple varieties of this tool can be found on the market for certain terrains and surfaces.

8. Shovel

A shovel seems to be the most common tool used, not only is this garden essential for digging but can be used for nearly anything garden related. As well as digging, removing and loosening of garden materials such as compost, fertiliser, soil, etc, can be a job for a spade.

9. Wheelbarrow

Any serious gardener will know the struggle of moving heavy and awkward materials around when out in the garden. To make this task easier, a wheelbarrow will allow you to load all materials and waste into its basket like a metal tray base, and wheel/transport it with ease to your designated area using its wheels.

10. Saw

Whether you're cutting a few branches/twigs off your shrubs or off a tree, a saw is the garden tool to use. Using its sharp rigid blade, a saw will see you through near enough any cutting tasks in the garden. Remember to choose a saw that suits your style as many different varieties of a saw are out there on the market.

CONCLUSION

This is simply, a list of the most important accessories one might need, for optimal growing circumstances. Every structure is different; due to the fact that it will be located within a unique climate, serve a different purpose, be used for growing different types of plants and be constructed with different materials. For most people, an excellent greenhouse garden can be achieved with just heaters for winter, shade cloth for the warmer months, manual or automatically opening ventilation window units, lights and a misting system.